SMALL BOAT RACING WITH THE CHAMPIONS

Edited by Bob Fisher

PRENTICE-HALL Inc.,
Englewood Cliffs, N.J.

© Barrie & Jenkins Limited 1976

First American Edition
published by Prentice-Hall Inc., 1977

First published in the UK by Barrie & Jenkins
in association with Bayard Books
and The Wordsmiths Company Limited

Printed in England by Jolly & Barber Ltd, Rugby.

Acknowledgement is made to the class associations and
others who kindly supplied information and assistance.

Library of Congress Catalog Card No: LC 76-16710

ISBN 0-13-814186-X

Contents

I believe that the phrase 'Vanity Time' will be added to the long list of sailing terms – a list going back in history. It was used by one of the twelve top 'artists' who Bob Fisher persuaded to expound their own ways of dealing with the problems of Championship sailing.

I have long known Bob Fisher afloat, both on the sea and in the clubhouse. I have envied his ability as a raconteur and respected his skill as a 'gamesman'. I enjoyed sailing against him as a world class helmsman. Where I feared him was as a crew, not, of course, in my boat, but in a competitor's boat. He has the unusual ability to add considerably to a helmsman's performance. He has carried more good helmsmen in different classes to Championship titles than anyone in post-war years.

It is this ability to get the best out of a number of different helmsmen, each Champion, often in more than one class, that has made him the ideal person to collect their various, and often differing, race winning ideas.

In this book, he has presented us with a unique opportunity to compare techniques. It must comfort ordinary sailors to find out that this collection of supermen agree with us that boats should be kept race-worthy but tend to differ, even amongst themselves, as to how best to win races.

One of the most interesting aspects of our sport is that one can, from time to time, sail against these Masters. It is nice to know that they all have our basic problems. They just work harder and solve them better.

I, for one, am grateful to Bob for collecting the facts and laying them out so well.

Beecher Moore.
Spring, 1976

This is not simply a book about *what* to do, because almost everybody who races boats has the basic knowledge necessary for some degree of success. Here, the acknowledged experts, sailors who between them have won more world and national championships than are held in any one year explain how they make progress in the class of their choice; not only how they get the best out of the boat itself, but how they use it against their rivals.

Boatspeed alone is useless. Crown Prince Harald of Norway, who had won Kiel Week 1972 easily, woefully explained his lowly performance a few months later at the Olympics: 'The trouble with good boatspeed is that if you go the wrong way you have a lot further to come back – I've got plenty of boatspeed, but no sense of the right direction in this Regatta.' Likewise, on its own, tactical ability cannot win races. It is possible for a slower boat to hold up a faster one, but not for long. It may be useful to hold up a rival to win a series, but that is likely to be when he has marked superiority in a certain weather condition and not in others.

The true measure of a champion is his ability to combine his efforts. To match good boatspeed with sound tactics is the only way to win races and to tie a series together. Championships are almost invariably decided by a series; only the International 14s, the oldest of the International dinghy classes, acclaim their champion on the results of a single race, and they do make it a very special one. Fortunately, it is possible to develop the ability to win races when the pressure is on.

Top sailors do not clam up about their technical and sporting ability, but only a few people get the chance to ask them the all-important questions which could improve their own performance. In the second part of this book, each of the twelve champions has been asked the same questions, except where they are irrelevant to their particular class. The answers to these questions on tactics are given in full, so it is easy to assess the comparative importance they attach to different techniques.

This is the first time that so many champions have together provided 'how-we-do-it' information, and their slightly differing methods of approach give the aspiring champion a choice. To succeed in dinghy and keelboat racing, it is essential not only to copy but also to develop the ideas of the current winners. The contents of this book, therefore, will help the reader to provide himself with a more than adequate base on which he can build. Following the champions directly will probably allow anyone to win races at club level – unless they have the champion to race against! From then on it is up to the individual.

One fact that does become apparent is the amount of time that the champions spend on preparing their boats and themselves for winning races. It is no use having a boat covered with all the necessary 'go-faster' fittings unless they work. Too often, the club sailor allows them to seize up, and then when he needs them they don't work. It is no use, either, having a boat with any projections on the bottom, or a rough surface on the rudder and centreboard. About these things every champion is agreed. And it is no use having a perfect boat if you cannot match it athletically. You must be able to sit out the whole of a heavy weather race and have enough in hand to do it all over again, if there are two races that day. These are the hallmarks of champions and become readily apparent from what the champions say.

The important thing about yacht-racing is to get as much enjoyment as possible from it. As enjoyment is often directly proportional to success, this book will, I hope, help you to succeed more and, therefore, to enjoy the sport more.

Chapter 1

Yacht-racing was once the province of the very rich. Yachts were huge, needed large crews of paid hands to tend them and were almost invariably steered by a professional skipper with the owner taken along as passenger. Quite often the owner did not even go afloat, treating his yacht as he would his string of race horses, as just another sporting toy, a whim to be indulged. They were raced for purses and the whole sport was quite different from the one that we know today. It was only after the First World War that small boat racing got under way. Even then it was viewed with some apprehension and disdain by the owners of the large yachts. However, it is small boat racing that has contributed most to the overall development of sailing boats, and ideas which make headlines when they appear in events such as the Admiral's Cup have often been seen in dinghies years before.

Small boat racing is now fully international. It is regarded as an athletic sport and has been included in the Olympic Games since 1900, although it was not until 1920 that true small boat racing received the ultimate accolade. Then racing for a 12-foot and an 18-foot centreboard boat was introduced, though these were nothing like the racing dinghies of today. Perhaps the real start of dinghy-racing came towards the end of the 1920s.

Until then there had been no concerted efforts made to race more than a few boats of the same type. Round the coast of England each club had its own particular design, and in the west the clubs got together to formulate a rule to which 14-foot dinghies could be built. In 1927 these boats became known as the International 14s. Recognition by the International Yacht Racing Union (IYRU) gave some respectability to dinghy-sailors and also the necessary impetus to spread the sport. In that same year the Prince of Wales gave a cup, to be raced for during the new class's championship week, and the seal of approval was finally set. In that first International 14s race for the Prince of Wales Cup forty-one boats entered the race. Thirty years later the entry was exactly the same, and it had never reached sixty boats. Today this doyen of the dinghy classes attracts close on a hundred entries, and, though it has its own particular appeal, it is not one of the dinghies which has achieved world-wide popularity.

The early racing dinghies were heavy, and it was not until 1928, when Uffa Fox produced *Avenger*, that a dinghy was made to plane. *Avenger* had a fantastic record, winning fifty-three of her fifty-seven races in her first season, yet writing of her later Uffa remarked that she was built on the light side; he had designed her to carry 11 square feet of sail less than the maximum allowed, 125 feet. At that time the rules required that if a boat weighed less than a certain amount she had to lose some sail area to race level. Obviously the rule-makers of those days understood what made a boat go fast!

Even so *Avenger* was built in a very traditional way with carvel planking, just like a small version of a big yacht, though Uffa Fox was one of the first to realize the advantages of other constructions. It was he, too, who did much of the early design development on dinghies, and during the dinghy boom after the Second World War he became one of the most prolific designers, a man whose skill and ingenuity in wood engineering earnt him immortal fame in the eyes of all small boat sailors. For what really enabled small boats to be built in any number was the development of resin glues and waterproof plywood during the Second World War. In 1945, Faireys, who had built fighter aeroplanes in wood, were left with their plant and nothing to do with it. For them Uffa designed several dinghies, the most successful of which, the *Firefly*, is still raced today in great numbers.

When it was first introduced the *Firefly* cost £60, but even this sum was too much for many of the people who wanted to race boats. At about the same time the editor of *Yachting World*, Teddy Haylock, commissioned a small dinghy for young people, which parents would be able to build at home without too much difficulty. For the design he went to Jack Holt, who was producing the designs for some National 12s and International 14s as well as all the early *Merlins*. Jack Holt was a practical man, too, and built the boats in his yard at Putney. Holt produced the *Cadet*, a hard-chined, pram-bowed dinghy 10 feet 6 inches long. Its success was immediate, not only because of its sailing capabilities, but also because of its ease of construction, and *Yachting World* soon followed it up with another Jack Holt design, the GP 14. Holt became the most prolific small boat designer and slowly developed his construction techniques with new designs over the years, *Yachting World* publishing most of them.

In 1931 the American yachting magazine *Rudder* published the design of a 15-foot 6-inch dinghy called the *Snipe*. Designed by Bill Crosby, the editor of the magazine, it was one of the first classes to achieve a truly international spread. Only recently it just failed to be chosen for the

International Cadet dinghies, the under-17s racing boat, the first ever do-it-yourself design published by Yachting World.

Olympics, and its list of past champions includes many of the great names of sailing. A total of twenty thousand *Snipes* were built in just over forty years, an impressive figure until one realizes that the *Laser* passed that total in only four years. In the forty years between the introduction of the *Snipe* and that of the *Laser* the sport of dinghy-racing has grown immensely.

One of the reasons for this growth was that the boats could be raced on small areas of inland water, and very soon not only rivers and lakes but flooded gravel-pits became regatta centres. Clubs mushroomed and many of those where dinghies are raced regularly and well were only formed after 1945. This growth was classless, in direct contrast to the early days of yacht-racing. Technological development was undoubtedly slower, however, and few entrepreneurs took advantage of the boom. Much of the gear and sails was simply scaled-down versions of those used on bigger boats. Fittings were heavy brass castings at best, but sometimes only galvanized iron was available. Clothes line pulleys were regularly used as mainsheet blocks, and stainless steel rigging was unheard of. The masts of many of the early *Cadets* were made from ex-government spruce oars.

Cotton sails meant hard work. If they got wet they shrank; if they got salt on them they remained damp and went out of shape. To win races sails had to be ironed beforehand, and a good deal of mystique attached itself to sailmaking. When new, the sails had to be stretched gently, by reaching up and down with them on a sunny day. Sailmakers had to estimate just how much the cotton cloth and the natural fibre bolt ropes would stretch. Thus the advent of terylene cloth and cordage in the early 1950s at last gave the sailmaker an even chance. This more stable material has very little stretch, and today there is more science and less 'art' in the production of sails.

Metal masts made their first appearance at about the same time as terylene. Though they had been part of the original *Firefly* specification, the idea did not take off for another ten years, the shortage of good-quality spruce for spars forcing their development as much as anything else. Twenty years later a wooden spar has become as rare as a metal one in the early 1950s. The bend characteristics of a metal mast remain the same no matter what the weather, while those of a spruce mast alter with the humidity. Once again sailmakers benefited, for they could cut sails to fit the spars in the certain knowledge that the spars would act the same way each time.

Glassfibre reinforced plastics (grp) was another new material that came into prominence at the same time. Because of the conservatism of all sailors, it took some time for grp boats to make much impression on the market. The first small dinghies looked like bathtubs, and potential owners did not like the idea of anything but wood. Designs were for wooden boats, and the new material did not adapt well to them. Flat sections which were amply stiff in plywood were hard to manufacture in grp without making the whole boat heavy. Some class associations at first forbade the use of grp, but eventually the barriers came down as grp technology improved. Boats were designed to be built in grp; this meant that the one-design concept could be more rigidly applied than ever before and boat building moved from traditional craftsmen working in small units towards factory production – to such an extent that one company with eight factories now supplies the world market with the most successful small racing boat ever designed. This is a far cry from the one-off builder who probably made no more than six boats of any one type before the design or decking layout was changed.

It was the revolutionary changes in boat building and equipment materials that made this dramatic growth possible. Behind it all, however, was a competitive desire to improve. Sailing became more a struggle of man against man rather than of boat against boat or purse against purse. As the boats improved so did sailing techniques. Racing dinghies became less an afternoon's outing, more a thoroughly competitive sport.

The first race for the Prince of Wales Cup in 1927 was sailed over a course that did not give one windward leg. Today race officers live in fear of shifting winds that move the mean wind more than 10 degrees from the line of the windward leg of the course. The first Prince of Wales Cup was held in highly tidal water off the mouth of the River Medina at Cowes with a line so biased that for success there was only one place to start (the leeward end of the line), for from there it was far less distance to sail, with a fair tide to do it in. Nowadays almost all the competitors scream if there is more than a few degrees of bias on a starting-line, and tidal waters are frowned upon.

This state of affairs persisted until the early 1960s, however. Class championships were held by clubs where a fleet of that class existed. It was considered something of a privilege for a club to be offered the championship, and for many years the smaller classes raced their championships around club courses starting from fixed lines. The more senior classes had begun to adopt the American method of starting, from a Committee Boat, and sailed around a

triangular course. In 1928 the International 14s sailed the POW around a triangular course; but there was still not a windward leg on it! It was another year before there was a beat in the POW course. Yet even then those who sailed the big racing yachts were aware that there was a great deal of skill in sailing a boat to windward, and most of the course in their races consisted of a beat and run; the 'soldier's wind' for reaching was left to the cruising fraternity.

Not until Uffa Fox designed *Avenger*, the International 14 that would plane, did reaching have any real purpose. Uffa made his boat light. His oft-quoted phrase 'weight only has value in a steamroller' is as true now as then. Planing is not just a matter of having a light boat and a good breeze but rather one of technique. Nowadays keelboats plane, given the right conditions and a helmsman who knows what he is about, and it is on the downwind legs of a course that the most significant differences in speed occur and the most dramatic place changes are made. These are the result of improvements in the technique of sailing as well as the more sophisticated machines that are now being sailed.

International competition racing

Jeremy Pudney and Richard Flek in a flat-out plane in the International 14 *Windchatter*. The 14 was the first dinghy to achieve international status.

remained unimportant for many years, not so much because no one wanted to race as because very different types of boats raced in different parts of the world. International racing always took place in borrowed boats, for it was not easy to transport the dinghies. The restriction on the hound height of the mast of the International 14, which persisted until 1976, was to permit the mast to be packed into a railway truck! A European Championship was held in the 1930s; the exploits of a youthful Stewart Morris, who won it for Britain in 1938, are recounted in Uffa Fox's *Thoughts on Yachts and Yachting*.

The last twenty-five years or so have seen a vast change in attitudes. One of the turning-points came at the 1948 Olympics when an unknown Dane called Paul Elvström won the Gold Medal in the singlehanded class. It was not so much that an unknown had won it but the way he went about winning it that surprised people. He had actually bothered to sail that sort of boat before entering for his national trials, and he had made sure that he was fit. When he found that by sitting out for longer periods than his rivals at the Olympics, he could beat them, Elvström realized that he would have to train for sailing in the same way that other athletes trained for their sports. Before the next Olympics, stories came out of

Denmark of this young man who trained at home on strange self-torture apparatus. He concentrated his efforts on holding a sitting-out position, training with a weight on his chest for a long time. But Elvström did not stop there. He spent as much time in his boat as possible so that everything he did became second nature. He made sure that he never funked a heavy weather gybe, his *Finn* was like an extension of his arms and legs. It was hardly surprising that in 1952, at Helsinki, Paul Elvström won his second Gold Medal.

After that the rest of the dinghy-sailing world gradually realized that there was no chance of success at the highest level without a certain amount of dedication to the sport. It had left the 'pastimes' category for ever and a revolution in attitudes had begun. As surely as Elvström had knocked aside the taboo of training for sailing, others tackled systematically each element essential for winning yacht races.

By now communications between sailors all over the world were improving and there were more international meetings. The International classes were keen to promote themselves and jet travel helped to make world championships possible all over the globe. It was no longer strange to think of the class's premier event being in Australia one year, America the next and Ireland the year after. The parochial viewpoint adopted by the English and later by the Europeans disappeared.

The consequences were felt at every level. Club sailors became aware of how the champions were dealing with their problems, of how they rigged their boats and the latest techniques for sailing them. It was easy for club sailors to copy and improve their performance at whatever level they chose to race. Thus standards improved and more and more people were drawn to higher levels of competition.

Suddenly, too, people became aware of the value of tactics, not just boat for boat tactics but also ways of dealing with the elements to the best advantage. Almost everyone was aware that if the wind headed when they were going to windward it paid them to tack, but it was all too easy to miss the windshift. Windshifts were easy enough to see when sailing towards the land where the heading could be assessed against a landmark. As courses went further off-shore sailors were faced with a problem. It was some time before compasses were used, at first only to pinpoint marks of the course, later as tactical weapons. Initially they were used for the upwind legs only, but it was not long before the

Lasers at the World Championship in Bermuda. The Laser is the growth phenomenon of the 1970s – close on 40,000 were built in the first 4 years.

top sailors realized their value on the runs as well and today a whole race can be planned around compass readings.

Small boat racing today is a scientific sport. Preparation of the boat is considered important by all who go afloat, and rarely is a boat sailed in the state in which it comes from the builder. It has to be adapted to fit its sailors and the way that they sail. All this has made the sport more expensive, but there are those who get as much enjoyment preparing their boats as in racing them; they are happy to think that they can win their races ashore, by having some minor advantage over their rivals. Gone are the days when there were significant advantages to be gained by thinking up a new way of dealing with gear problems or by having a very different sail, cut just within the rules. It once worked for me; in the *Fireball* class I had the first jib cut with the clew almost on the deck. I produced it for the World Championship amidst a very sceptical bunch of rivals. After a couple of races they realized that I had the drop on them, for I was either able to point 5 degrees higher or free off and foot on

the same course as them but 5 per cent faster. Breakthroughs like that are few and far between, and fewer than ever now.

To win Olympic medals demands rapid thinking, a high level of co-ordination and physical fitness. The last cannot be too heavily stressed. When Keith Musto and Tony Morgan went to the Tokyo Olympics and gained a Silver Medal in the *Flying Dutchman* class, they were described by Desmond Hackett in the *Daily Express* as the fittest athletes in the British team; and Hackett meant the whole team, including the track and field athletes.

To win club races is a little less demanding, but it does need 100 per cent concentration, and it gets more difficult every time. The open meeting circuit sailors have a slightly bigger problem in winning races, because their competition is stronger. To get the most out of the sport it is best to fix one's level and stay within it. If you improve, there is always a higher standard to aspire to or another class to try. There is something for everyone.

505

Peter White

Chapter 2

World Champion 1973; 6th, World Championships 1974 and 1975; 3rd, European Championship 1973; 2nd, British National Championships 1972 and 1974. Sailmaker.

The *505* was designed by John Westell of Britain after a series of IYRU trials that selected the *Flying Dutchman* as the boat for international two-man racing. In these trials a similar boat, *Coronet,* came close to being selected. The *505* was commissioned by the Caneton Association of France to replace the elderly hard-chine *Caneton.* There are now almost six thousand world-wide, and the class steadfastly refuses to campaign for Olympic selection, although in the eyes of many dinghy sailors it is a far better boat than the *Flying Dutchman.* Now twenty-one years old, the design is still ahead of its time.

Length: 5050 mm
Beam: 1880 mm
Sailarea: 14·5 sq m (main and jib), 19·97 sq m (spinnaker)
Weight: 127·01 kg (minimum, all up)

As a sailmaker I am perhaps biased when I say that the rig is the most important factor for good boatspeed in the *505* class. It is more correct to say that boatspeed relies on a combination of correct rig, good hull with perfect centreboard and rudder, and the people who sail the boat. Good boatspeed is the result of getting all the factors working together.

Stiffness, weight distribution and finish are the three most important factors in the hull, and the only way to get all three right is through close consultation with the builder. Naturally the hull must be down to the minimum weight allowed by the class; nothing stops a boat more quickly than carrying excess weight. In the *505* class we are lucky that there are hardly any restrictions on the construction of the boat, and we can, therefore, use the newest materials to suit the requirements of the boat. The hull shape is fairly tightly controlled, and few people have bothered to exploit the tolerances; those who have tried have not produced a boat significantly faster in any single condition, let alone a good all-round boat.

The shape of the hull lends itself to good fibreglass construction, and there are sufficient good builders available to improve the breed constantly. Wood has not proved popular, although there is little doubt that a well-engineered wooden boat is every bit as fast as a glass one – people in the *505* class are happier sailing their boats than working on them. Since carbon fibre is regularly used to stiffen glassfibre *505*s, and experiments with Kevlar are well underway, the reinforced plastics hull

Spinnaker reaching at the 1973 World Championship in Hong Kong.

has everything to recommend it.

It is necessary to triangulate the structure around the mast and the shrouds and forestay so that it remains as rigid as possible. It is not only important to stop the shrouds and forestay from compressing inwards under load but also to stop the mast from pushing the bottom of the boat downwards. This triangular structure is firmly fixed to the centreboard case, and the whole forms the basic framework over which the *505* is built. The forward part of the skin must also be very stiff to take the pounding of the waves, and careful use of carbon fibre in this area helps enormously; care must also be taken to keep the weight out of the bow. The amount of glass mat and resin should be lessened towards the two ends of the boat.

Both centreboard and rudder should be stiff, well shaped and have a good finish. Most *505* builders have a special marine plywood made for them for centreboards, with most of the veneers running in one direction. This is excellent and is only rivalled by laminated hardwood boards. Good shape means a rounded leading-edge aerofoil with the maximum chord at about 45 per cent. It then tapers to a squared-off back edge of $\frac{1}{8}$ of an inch thick. The same is true for the rudder blade. In the *505* a gybing centreboard that goes about 3 degrees away from the centreline does seem to work, although there are other sailors at the front of the fleet who prefer a very rigid board that does not flop about at all in the case. The rigid board comes into its own in heavier weather.

To get a good finish on the centreboard and rudder I use two-part polyester paint, white of course, which I rub down between each of the eight to ten coats, finally burnishing it with 400 grade wet-and-dry sandpaper. After each time afloat the centreboard and rudder should be examined and any nicks or chips repaired.

The rudderhead must be strong, to take the strains on it, but it must also be light. The blade of a lifting rudder must be a tight fit in the head, and if you are racing regularly in deep water without shallows it is well worth having a fixed rudder. The blade must be big enough to allow full control of the boat on tight spinnaker reaches.

A stiff hull is essential for setting up a modern *505* rig. The mast has to be strong enough yet light. With the spreaders set up (I use fixed spreaders which deflect the shrouds slightly forward of their normal line), the maximum mast bend in the fore and aft plane should be $4\frac{1}{2}$ inches measured in the middle of the mast. The shroud height is not restricted, and in order to stiffen the topmast laterally the anchorages for the shrouds have crept higher. Eighteen inches above the forestay is the reasonable maximum, any higher and a lot of pre-bend is induced in the mast by the forestay when the shrouds are set up tight. This can be partially overcome with forward-deflecting spreaders but a balance between the two appears to be best. The lateral stiffness is important to support the mainsail leech.

The boom I use is the lightest I can obtain, but not necessarily the stiffest. Here I may be wrong, but I believe that in the stronger winds the ability of the boom to bend helps to free the leech of the large mainsail that the *505* carries. The spinnaker pole, on the other hand, must be as strong as possible and light. With the big *505* kite it is important that the pole does not ride up, and a good hook and eye system is the best for the vang. I don't like the permanently-rigged pole systems which 'fly-away' along the boom since they seem to provide an awful lot of windage on the upwind legs. I make no provision for altering the pole height, but I do carry a lightweight set of sheets for the spinnaker.

There is no need to have several different suits of sails to win in the *505*. I use only one mailsail and jib for a regatta but have two spinnakers, the lightweight one for the very light winds. It is far more important to have sails which can be adjusted by altering the

rig. In light airs sails must be set close to the centreline of the boat with the jib sheeted well down the leech and the mainsail set with a small amount of twist. To do this the mainsheet traveller is pulled up to windward and the sheet eased. In medium winds the jib fairlead is moved aft a small amount so that the top of the leech may twist off and cut down the backwinding of the mainsail. The mainsail leech is tightened and the twist taken out by using more mainsheet tension and by moving the traveller into the centre of the track. In light and medium winds the mast must be firmly chocked at the deck. Only $1\frac{1}{2}$ inches of play at the deck are needed when the wind is strong. This will allow the mast to bend to the maximum $4\frac{1}{2}$ inches. The jib leads should be moved outboard to open the slot as the wind increases, for the mainsail will also be further out and will otherwise choke the slot. By pulling out the foot to the black band and tightening down on the cunningham the flow of the sail is moved forward and the sail is flattened; also, the leech is freed. The kicker has to be tightened so that the mainsheet has very little effect on the leech tension.

Because of the 6-foot 6-inch beam of the *505*, there is a lot of righting power available from the crew, and so I have my sails cut full to take advantage of this. Weight jackets are allowed in this class and they should be worn

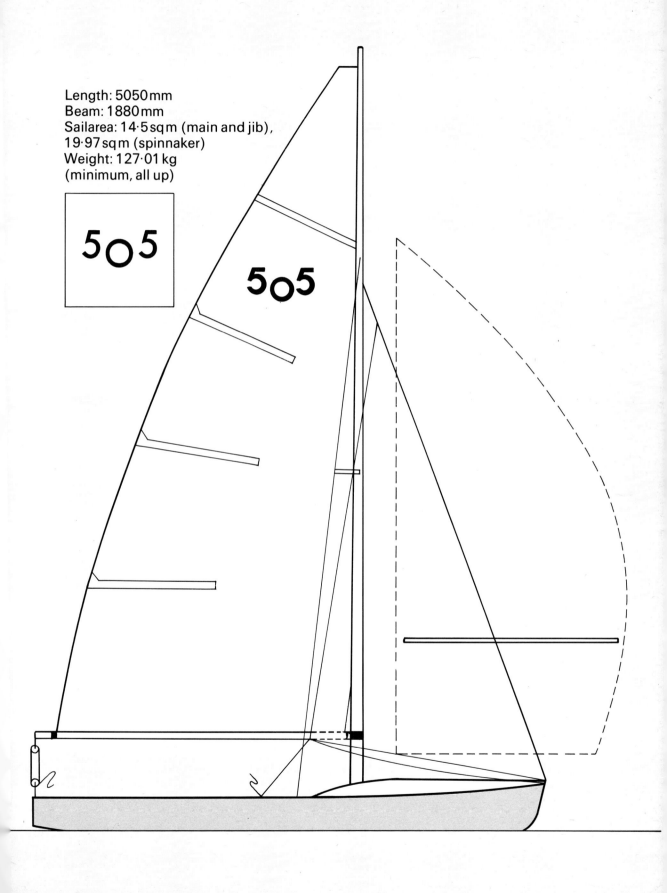

Length: 5050 mm
Beam: 1880 mm
Sailarea: 14·5 sq m (main and jib),
19·97 sq m (spinnaker)
Weight: 127·01 kg
(minimum, all up)

5○5

when racing in stronger breezes. They are so important that it is worth having two sets so that the driest, and therefore the lightest, is taken afloat for every race just in case the wind gets up. Full-cut sails will provide all the power necessary for the reaches. When there are stronger winds it does appear worthwhile to free off the kicking strap on the main boom, on the shy spinnaker reaches, to spill wind out of the top of the mainsail, still keeping the driving power on in the lower half of the sail.

All the controls for the sails should be led to the gunwale, and they must be kept as simple as possible so that they have a good chance of functioning properly. Colour coding the lines is important but particularly with a new boat, there is no substitute for marking what each line does, either with a Dymo strip or by painting the name on the deck. It saves thinking time.

To go fast the skipper must be comfortable and can only be so if the toe-straps are properly adjusted. There is no fixed, correct place for them – it depends on the leg length of every individual helmsman. They must also be held up so that, after a tack, the helmsman does not have to look for them to get his feet under.

The most important single factor to contribute to success in the *505* is good teamwork and total understanding between helmsman and crew. This takes time and practice to achieve and is helped by physical fitness and by wearing the right gear, so that both helmsman and crew are warm and comfortable. But teamwork is the keynote.

Derek Farrant with Bev Moss on the wire, powering away from a start. Speed is essential at this time in the race, in these heavy seas, to get clear wind.

Flying Dutchman

Rodney Pattisson

Chapter 3

Olympic Gold Medallist 1968 and 1972; World Champion 1969, 1970, 1971; European Champion 1968, 1970 and 1975.

The *Flying Dutchman* was chosen as an International racing class in 1954 after trials over two years. At first it did not display any real superiority, but additional sailarea in the form of the genoa made a great difference. Today the class prospers all over the world; it has already appeared at four Olympics, has been chosen for the fifth, and seems unlikely to be replaced in the near future. It is a big boat by the standards of most dinghies and has a great deal of initial stability, but its performance both upwind and down, in light or heavy conditions, is sparkling. Good crewing is at a premium in the *Flying Dutchman*, and the speed differential between a well-handled boat and a less well-sailed rival is enormous.

Length: 6050 mm
Beam: 1720 mm
Sailarea: 18·85 sq m (main and jib), 17·65 sq m (spinnaker)
Weight: 165·11 kg (minimum)

I find it very difficult to compare all the factors that control the boatspeed of the *Flying Dutchman*, for every one is inter-related. A boat as responsive as the *Flying Dutchman* has to be cared for more than any other, since one thing

Jean-Marie Danielou at WOW 1975.

wrong can result in a disastrous performance. The speed differentials are enormous and in top-class racing you cannot afford to give away an inch. That inch may mean the difference between getting an overlap at a buoy, and not getting it, or, worse still, being overlapped unnecessarily and losing a great deal more. When I won my first Gold Medal, I had boatspeed to spare. I had been pushed hard for the selection for the British place at Acapulco by John Oakeley, who had until then reigned supreme in the class internationally, and this meant that I had to have everything perfect. As a result, it was probably easier winning the Gold than being selected for Britain!

I learnt early the importance of boatspeed in the *Flying Dutchman* class, and by experimenting with the secondhand boat that I first had I was able to assess what made the boat go faster. More than anything, I believe that you must have the correct shape. The tolerances allowed in the International *Flying Dutchman* class rules are sufficient to permit very different shapes to be built into the hull of the boat. The builders are aware of this and will have made every effort to measure accurately the fastest boats on the circuit. They also benefit from the opinions of their better customers, who will tell them how they want their boats built; they will probably have measured another fast boat and then think that they can produce an even faster one with some slight modification. And in this game it is no use just copying; you have to improve on the best available in order to beat the other man.

For many years I have been lucky to be associated with Bob Hoare, who has built all my *Flying Dutchmen*. We discuss what should be done, and somehow Bob seems to manage to transfer my ideas perfectly into the wooden hull. Once the shape is fixed the builder has no tolerance to work to and has to ensure that the hull is perfectly fair. That, perhaps more than anything else, is the secret of good boatspeed. A great deal of energy is dissipated in forcing the hull through the water, and there is no point in wasting energy by forcing the water to go a greater distance by having a hull that is all bumps and hollows. It takes not only a great deal of hard work to get the hull lines of a *Flying Dutchman* fair but also a lot of skill – a job best left to the craftsmen. It is not beyond the ability of the amateur but there is always the chance that in trying to fair the hull you will go too far and alter the desired shape.

The shape that I am currently using is the result of all my years of experience with the class. Naturally I have altered my ideas as a result of my own performance and that of others, and I am always looking for ways to improve the hull. Some boats are always faster downwind for instance, and I think this is not so much because of their rigs or the way they are sailed as because of the shape of the hull.

It is also important to get the hull as stiff as possible and to keep the weight out of the ends; the stiffer the hull and the more the weight is concentrated into the middle, the more lively the boat, and you should go to the very limits of the rules in this respect. Large areas of the aft deck can be cut away and replaced with thin plastic sheet 'inspection hatches'. The same can be done on the foredeck where these hatches are necessary to gain access to the jib furling gear to service it. Both the skin and the supporting structure must be stiff. It is no use going to great lengths to tie the shroud anchorages in with the mast so that the whole strain of the rig is carefully taken in a triangu-lated structure if the hull pants in between the frames. Stiff means totally stiff.

The hull must be minimum weight: nothing else is acceptable. It must also have a perfect finish.

I prefer to use wooden centre-boards and rudders because they are easy to finish and to keep in good condition. Wood covered with glass-fibre is always a problem; it is hard to get a perfect bond between the wood

Length: 6050 mm
Beam: 1720 mm
Sailarea: 18·85 sq m (main and jib),
17·65 sq m (spinnaker)
Weight: 165·11 kg (minimum)

FD

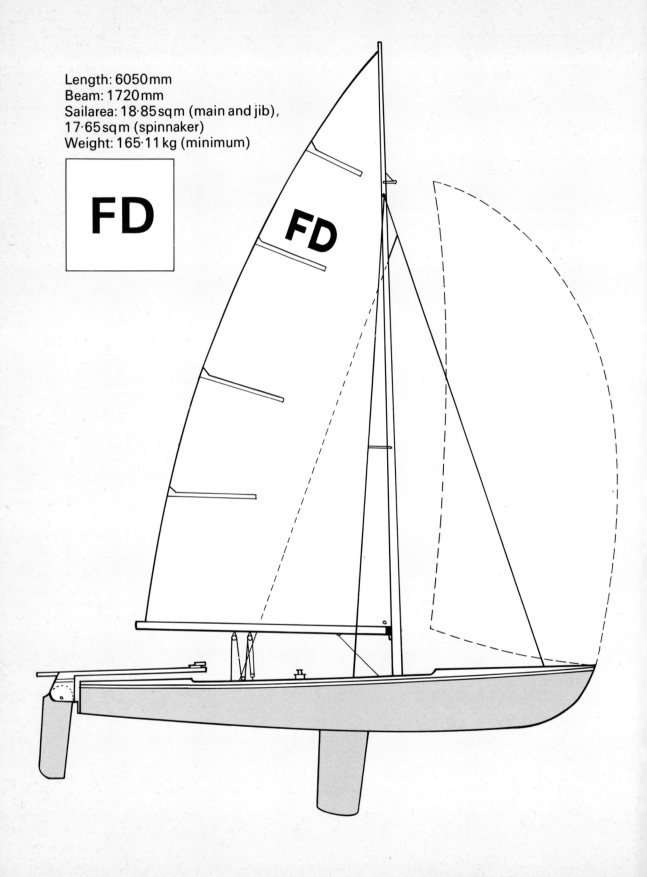

and the glass and almost impossible to stop the damp getting in after a knock. Glassfibre covered boards also turn out heavier and give negligible additional stiffness. A springy wood such as mahogany is better than teak, which is very 'dead', although it is worth using teak for the leading and trailing edges. Both the centreboard and rudder should be made of laminated strips with the laminates reversed alternately to prevent the finished board from warping. One word of warning: if you do use a teak strip for the leading and trailing edge it must be cleaned of oil with a solvent before gluing. Any paints other than two-part polyurethane or epoxy are useless for the final finish as this must be glass hard before it is finally burnished.

The rig provides power and must be as efficient as it can be made. I am horrified by the way some people throw away potential boatspeed through obvious inefficiencies in their rigs; they are rarely found at the front of the fleet at the end of a race. The rig must be tuned to the weight of each individual crew and for this it is important to have a mast with the right bend characteristics and spreaders which can control the amount of bend.

The Elvström *Flying Dutchman* mast most nearly approaches perfection. It is as narrow sideways as is possible and its top is tapered so that in a strong breeze it flexes sideways and frees off the leech at the head of the mainsail; this takes out the heeling moment of the rig in the most efficient manner while keeping the drive in the mainsail low down. By moving the angle of the spreaders forward the mast can be made stiffer in the fore and aft plane. The Elvström mast has all the shroud anchorages inside, cutting down the windage to a bare minimum. I go even further and fair in the spreader anchorages and sheave cages with a fibreglass paste. The last thing you want is anything that gets in the way of the air flow around the sails.

Ideally the mast of the *Flying Dutchman* should have correct flexibility, and minimum section and weight. The boom should be as light and stiff as possible; with a flexible topmast there is no need for the boom to bend to free the mainsail leech.

All the gear for the spinnaker must be easily worked. The pole should be of the minimum weight permitted and a spare should be kept in the boat. As you have to carry a paddle in the *Flying Dutchman* there is no reason why the spare spinnaker boom should not be made into the paddle. It is essential to carry the spare, for it is easy enough to drop the spinnaker boom overboard and lose a lot of time returning for it. It is also illegal to set a spinnaker without a boom, and just occasionally spinnaker

booms break. The end fittings should be controllable with one hand. I also think it important to be able to control the height of the outboard end of the pole when the spinnaker is set. To do this I have a not-too-complicated system using a drum and axle winch at the foot of the mast with a wire vang. With an endless rope on the drum I can alter the pole height at will.

The cut of the sails is a matter for discussion with the sailmaker, who will want to know what spars the sails are to be set on and the weight of the helmsman and crew. It is no use going to a sailmaker who does not know the finer points of the class, and so I tend to go to those who race *Flying Dutchmen*. Admittedly, trends do alter, but time and time again I return to the acknowledged all-round style that has been proved over and over again. I am not one of those who think you can win with one suit of sails in all weathers; the sails of the *Flying Dutchman* are big, and a lot of alteration is possible in the aerofoil shape, more in fact than can be accomplished with the draft controls found in the boat. This means that three suits of sails are best, for light, medium and heavy winds, and these have to be

Rodney Pattisson crewed by Iain Macdonald-Smith after gybing at the wing mark, at Poole Bay Olympic Week, 1967. John Oakeley is ahead but note the slickness of the gybe – one length from the mark, the spinnaker is drawing and Macdonald-Smith is now fixing the spinnaker pole to the mast.

adjusted to suit the variations of the wind within the particular range. A really light spinnaker is important for those days when the wind hardly blows at all, and this should be set on separate, ultra-light sheets.

Setting the sails correctly is even more important. In light winds the mainsail should be set with a slack leech with the mainsheet traveller in the centreline, giving a fair amount of twist to the mainsail. The jib is sheeted close in, again with a slack leech. In medium winds the leech of the mainsail is tightened by kicking-strap tension and the traveller is eased down the track. The twist is then taken out of the sail. The jib is sheeted further outboard with the leech quite tight. The important thing about the *Flying Dutchman's* rig, with its big overlap in the form of the genoa, is to get the slot between the main and the jib the same width all the way up. In strong winds the leech of the mainsail is kept tight until it is necessary to spill some wind, when it is slackened by the top of the mast bending sideways. The mainsheet traveller is slightly further outboard. The jib is also sheeted further outboard to prevent the slot from becoming choked. The leech is kept fairly tight but balances the shape of the mainsail.

The most important factor in maintaining boatspeed is to be able to set the boat up in exactly the same way each time. To do this every control must be calibrated, including the mainsheet and the jib sheets. All the controls must lead to the helmsman's hand as he is sitting out. The ideal is for the boat to become an extension of the skipper's arms and legs; then good boatspeed will be the norm.

International Moth

Chris Eyre

Chapter 4

British National Champion 1969, 2nd,
1970; 4th, European Championship
1973. Designer of Lucky Sixpence,
National Champion 1968; 2nd Nervous
Breakdown, National Champion 1969;
Sprite, National Champion and 2nd,
World Championship 1971; Poacher,
European Champion 1973.

The *Moth* is an open development class
with loose parameters. The rules restrict
only length, beam and sailarea; shape is
the province of the designer. As a result
there are many shapes racing, yet they
compete on equal terms. Some of the
basic shapes are better in certain
weather conditions, and the search
continues for the best all-round boat.

Length: 3355mm (maximum)
Beam: 2250mm (maximum)
Sailarea: 8sqm

I believe it is essential to keep the
controls of a *Moth* as simple as possible
in order to leave the helmsman the
maximum amount of time to
concentrate on sailing this sensitive
boat. The *International Moth* is a
difficult boat to sail well, and therefore
distractions should be minimized so
that the helmsman can get maximum
boatspeed from his outfit. The *Moth*
presents other problems, too, because it
is a development class with very few
restrictions on the design of the hull and
rig; it is surprising how, within this

3303 (Mervyn Cook) holding the ideal defensive
position while reaching over 3099 (Ross Ellison).

loose framework, boats of very different
shapes with highly differing rigs are
sailed against each other at closely
similar speeds. In a development class
the hull and rig are the most important
factors for boatspeed. In the early
1970s rigs have been developed more
than hulls, though during the 1960s the
converse was true.

It is an old adage that there is
nothing new under the sun in yacht
design, and in the *International Moth*
class this is all too patently true. John
Shelley from New Zealand designed a
boat in the mid-1960s that had a long
straight entry, flat rocker and a flat hard-
chined stern. In its various updated
forms this design was sailed
competitively until the early 1970s,
when, suddenly, the cognoscenti
declared it out-of-date. In 1974 Colin
Walker launched his Wakehurst design
with much the same shape and began to
win races in top competition. Perhaps
fashion more than anything else
dictates whether designs are out-of-
date!

In both the northern and southern
hemispheres, most modern *Moths* are of
a flat rockered wedge shape with a flat
'U' section throughout a very long entry.
They have a short parallel after-section
and probably represent the ultimate
development in Shelley's original ideas.
Their design has gone as far as it can
without turning the helmsman into a

waterborne acrobat, and the 'wedge' style has come into its own since lightweight rigs set in the right place in the boat have begun to appear. The *Magnum,* designed by Mervyn Cook, has the high aspect ratio, fully-battened rig set on a lightweight mast more than 3 feet from the bow. The result is that the driving forces are all located over the hull's centre of buoyancy, thus substantially reducing the pitching moment in rough water, a problem that was always present in the early Shelley designs.

Belief in the wedge-shaped hull is not total, and many of my rivals are still sailing well-established designs varying from the almost legendary round-bilged Duflos design that has won countless World and Continental championships, to the tunnel-hulled scows which reigned unchallenged in the southern hemisphere for eight years in the 1960s. The 'skiff' type of hull now falls into three categories: the round-bilged, the hard-chine and the narrow-gutted. The round-bilged is mainly derived from the Duflos, with improvements to make it easier to build; the *Mistral* is a good example of this type. In the hard-chined field, two designs tend to dominate, the *Sprite* and the later *Chelsea Morning.* The narrow-gutted boats owe much to Sean Cox and Peter Conway, who persist with these difficult-to-sail boats. There are many hybrids. My own

Poacher design is a round-bilged/ narrow-gut crossbreed aimed at all-round performance, with special emphasis on windward work in rough water.

The shape of a *Moth* hull can have a dramatic effect on performance in specific conditions. A scow hull will not perform well in light weather unless it is sailed heeled to about 15 degrees; a Duflos or any other light-weather design will not go well in rough conditions unless it is sailed very upright. Both are extremely difficult to manage and winning races is thus much easier for those who are sailing the hull designs most suitable for the prevailing wind and water conditions. This is why I and others have persisted in our attempts to achieve good all-round hull shapes and perhaps it also explains why the wedge type is currently very fashionable.

Once the design has been settled, and this remains a matter of the helmsman's own preference, how the boat is built is not so important. Some criteria must be observed, however. The *Moth* hull must be reasonably fair in shape and care must be taken to avoid knuckles and hollows. It is best to keep the hull as light as possible, and the careful builder can save valuable ounces by using wood engineering to the full. Once built the hull must be effectively sealed so that there is no chance of water soaking into it and putting on unnecessary weight.

I try to keep centreboards and rudder blades as light and stiff as possible. Mine are made from laminated obeche with oak or utile edges to provide protection for the brittle obeche. The blades are sealed with thinned varnish and painted to a high finish with white enamel. The paint is allowed to dry for two weeks and is then burnished to a silk smooth finish with 400 grade wet-and-dry sandpaper. The profile and section are of great importance. The profile I use for the centreboard follows the De Havilland shape tank-tested in Australia in the 1960s and has a trailing tip. The rudder is spade-shaped with maximum area at the foot and a minimum chord where it pierces the surface. The sections are rounded front aerofoils with the maximum thickness of chord at 50 per cent, tapering as straight as possible to a squared-off trailing edge of $\frac{1}{8}$ of an inch.

The mast must perform correctly its duty of supporting the sail in perfect shape in all weathers. It must also be as light as possible and must present the smallest frontal area possible. In heavy weather it must flex to leeward and aft at the top so that when the boat becomes overpowered the leech is freed and the sail feathered progressively. In order to do this I use a Sparlight DQ2 section supported with the hounds at just above half height and a rigid tripod spreader system with adjustment on the forestay spreader. This allows total control of the mast bend characteristics. The boom must be light yet rigid to allow accurate control of the sail camber at the outhaul and the leech tension imposed by the kicking strap. Present thinking favours a fully-battened sail that is almost flat when the mast bend has taken out the curvature along the luff, the camber of the sail being entirely induced by producing a conical flow shape with an efficient foot control. For this reason the outhaul must work in both directions when under full load from the mainsheet and kicker, and be controllable by the helmsman when sitting out. Masts are normally kept in their fully bent shape in all weathers by the kicking strap.

Setting the sail of a *Moth* becomes less of a problem when the system has been properly sorted out. I use a sleeve luff (wrapped round the mast) sail in lighter winds only. It is also probably more efficient in stronger winds than the more conventional sail hoisted in the luff groove, but I think that the practical considerations of hoisting the sleeve luff sail in strong winds, to say nothing of the safety problems involved in righting a boat with the sleeve full of water and the virtual impossibility of getting the sail down afloat, easily outweigh any advantages it may have.

Length: 3355 mm (maximum)
Beam: 2250 mm (maximum)
Sailarea: 8 sqm

The sail is set in much the same manner in all weathers; the adjustments for the force of the wind are carried out underway. The outhaul is pulled out to flatten the sail progressively when sailing to windward as the strength of the wind increases. It is eased to make the sail very full offwind in all breezes. The exception to this is in very, very light weather, when the camber is reduced upwind.

Luff tension may sometimes be increased slightly to remove the creases from the lower parts of the sail when the wind is really strong. Then the sail is also sheeted further out on the mainsheet traveller in heavy winds and rough water, in order to maintain rapid progress to windward.

Gear should be kept as simple as possible. There are five important things to remember: the outhaul system must be free running and readily adjustable. There must be a track for the mainsheet so that the rig can be feathered off in heavy weather when going to windward. The tripod spreader system has to have the forward stay adjustable to control the mast bend. The kicking strap controls the leech tension of the sail and should be readily adjustable. Finally, there must be an efficient bailer to keep the boat dry and light. With all these, sailing a *Moth* becomes less difficult and winning races a lot easier.

John Claridge (K 3583) leads John Pierce (K 3584) at the European Championship in Switzerland, 1975. Both are sailing Mervyn Cook-designed Magnums. Note the light weather, sleeve luffed sail used by Claridge with its high roach, and the all weather sail used by Pierce.

Soling

John Oakeley

Chapter 5

British Olympic representative in the *Soling* class at 1972 Games; winner of seventeen championships in various classes including the National, European and World championships of the *Flying Dutchman* Sailmaker.

The *Soling* has undoubtedly taken over from the *Dragon* as the three-man keel boat for international racing. Its physical demands on the crew have introduced a new dimension into keel-boat racing; they have to hike the boat in all but the lightest winds, though the introduction of mini-harnesses has relieved them of the arduous, spine-cracking sitting-out and allowed them more chance to contribute to sailing the boat, both in sail trim and in tactical decisions. The *Soling* is a highly responsive boat with a great deal of sailarea and big spinnakers; sail trim and instinctive reaction are of paramount importance for good boatspeed. First chosen for the Olympics in 1972, the *Soling* looks set for a long run in the Games.

Length: 8185mm
Beam: 1900mm
Sailarea: 21·7sqm
Weight: 1035kg

It is the perfect combination of hull, rig, keel and rudder that makes for a fast *Soling*. If any one of these is not perfect in itself, then the boat will not be fast,

National Champion Charles Ingham on his way to victory at WOW 1975.

for, since *Solings* are as alike as possible, it is attention to detail that makes for boatspeed; and without boatspeed, winning races in a *Soling* is totally impossible. A *Soling* crew has three members, which does help to spread the workload, but it is a big boat and even rubbing down the bottom is a time-consuming job.

The fastest hull is one in which the weight distribution is good. There are limitations on weight in the *Soling* rules, and it is therefore imperative to go to a builder who understands the construction rules intimately and who has experience of racing in the class; this limits the choice to Elvström in Denmark or Abbott in Canada. Both of these aim to keep the weight out of the ends, which is one of the most important things about a *Soling* hull. My second *Soling*, which was built by Elvström, felt far different from and was definitely faster than my original boat, which came from a British yard which no longer produces them; this was because the original one was overweight in the forward and after sections, although the total hull weight was close to the minimum allowed by the class rules.

The surface finish of the topsides and bottom of the hull also has a considerable effect on the speed of the boat. The finish should be smooth but matt. Some people think that the finish should resemble that of very fine sandpaper; one friend of mine many years ago varnished his *Firefly* in the lee of a coal tip and discovered that it had been covered with a very fine powder. His record in the championship week which followed was five firsts in five races! Nonetheless I prefer a perfectly smooth finish.

Because they are working under pressure all the time, the keel and rudder must be perfectly fair; their surface finish is far more important than that of the hull. They should be checked regularly and any nicks or dents must be filled in with Plastic Padding and rubbed down to match the surrounding area. Little can be done about their shape, except to make them perfectly fair and to see that the keel is placed as far aft as the tolerances allow.

The ideal mast must have a reasonable, aerodynamic shape, be as light as possible for a given stiffness, and fully controllable. *Soling* masts have tended to be bendy, with the spreaders fixed at right angles to the centreline and the main shrouds fixed at the deck. In the earlier rigs the spreaders were swinging and the main shrouds ran in tracks along the deck. Now only the lower shrouds should be movable in the fore and aft plane. The forestay should be adjustable to take up the full travel allowed by the backstay. It should have a stopperknot in the

forestay system so that when it is fully let off the boom end just clears the deck with the mainsheet hard in.

The mast should be set up before each race and the bottle screws on each of the shrouds adjusted so that they are the same length. If the lower shrouds are too tight they will pull the middle of the mast up to windward and help the top to fall off. This becomes more pronounced if the upper shrouds are too loose. The optimum tensions in the shrouds vary in different wind strengths, and only by sighting up the back edge of the mast when the boat is sailing to windward can the correct settings be judged. For sailing to windward in light winds use the maximum mast rake possible. As the wind strengthens the mast should become more upright. This will help to reduce the weather helm. Remember that all the time the rudder is not on the centreline it is applying a brake.

Windage, or rather lack of it, is all important on the mast and rigging. Few people realize that windage causes leeway. Windage can be reduced relatively easily, though it does take a little time. Do not leave screw heads showing, reduce the amount of tape used at the spreader ends, fair in the spreader base with the mast with Plastic Padding, attach the shrouds internally, cut down the size of the halyard shackles and make sure that

Length: 8185 mm
Beam: 1900 mm
Sailarea: 21·7 sqm
Weight: 1035 kg

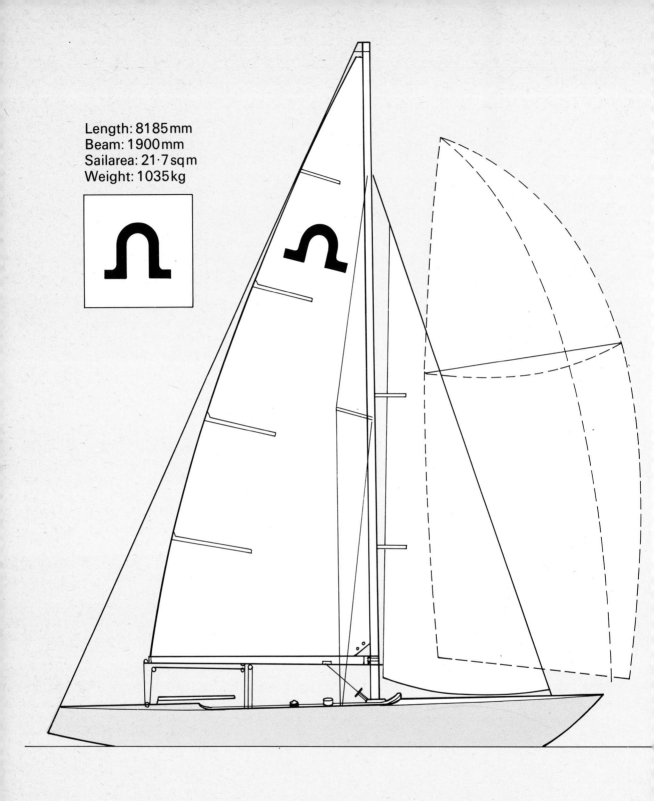

anything on the outside of the mast must be there. The spinnaker boom lift must be of wire. It takes very little ingenuity and imagination to be able to get the same effect and reduce the windage by at least three-quarters.

The heel of the mast is another area all too often overlooked. The heel must fit tightly on to the deck plate so that there is no rotation whatsoever. Even the slightest amount of rotation will upset the effect of the spreaders. This is a fault which creeps up as the season goes on and should therefore be checked every weekend.

The ideal boom should have as large a section and be as light as possible. The bigger the section, the better the 'end plate' effect it has. A boom with a flat-topped section produces this effect much better than an oval or round one. Whether or not the boom is bendy depends on personal preference; mine is for a boom that has some bend with a centre mainsheet. Recently there has been a tendency to aft mainsheeting, and almost without exception the boats that favour this system have won in light airs, though when the winds are stronger centre-mainsheet boats have the edge. It seems that the automatic feathering of the leech provided by the centre mainsheet and the slightly bendy boom helps the *Soling's* speed. In lighter weather the ability of the aft sheeting to

hold the leech of the mainsail in a rigid state gives more speed to windward. I am toying with what may be the final solution, fitting both types of sheeting so that either can be used after a minor, rapid change.

The best spinnaker system is the one that does the job it is supposed to do efficiently, with the minimum of effort. It must be light and be relied on to take the heavy strains imposed on it when the wind blows hard, as must the carriage on the mast with which the spinnaker boom is hoisted. It is important to be able to control the height of the outboard end of the spinnaker boom, particularly if the wind becomes light. All the cleats for the adjustable parts of the system should lead to the forward consol in the cockpit so that they are available for the forward hand who has to deal with them. Each control should have identification marks so that settings may be recorded and repeated.

The secret of sail shape has been puzzling me, along with every other competitor in yacht-racing, for years. Experiments using wind tunnels have attempted to solve the unknowns in shape and sheeting angles, but so far no one has come up with a definitive conclusion. Many people have come up with the same solutions after theoretical experiments, yet when these are applied to actual boats, they do not

have the desired effect. Everyone has a chance of solving the problems, and answers will not be found by blindly accepting the ideas of the winner. There is only one way to get better boatspeed and that is to think for yourself. Base your ideas on those of the experts, but make sure that you improve on them.

Mainsails on *Solings* have a slacker leech than those on dinghies, although the current trend is for a tighter leech in light weather. With the rig of a *Soling* it is possible to ease the leech of the mainsail to suit the conditions by tightening the backstay. Very little extra tension is needed on the backstay to free the leech quite considerably. In heavy weather the *Soling* reacts best if its sails are cut reasonably full, though the fullness should be well forward, about 25 to 30 per cent of the chord. In lighter weather the sails are best a little flatter with the fullness further aft, though this is contrary to dinghy practice.

To get the best out of the sails, your prime concern should be to ensure that the angle of attack along the luff is constant with the wind direction; remember this is not the same all the way up the sail.

With the jib it is easy to adjust the

Approaching the weather mark, spinnaker poles already set. Holland's Gert Bakker is to weather of Stuart Walker of the United States at the 1973 World Championship.

sheet position in the clew plate and the position of the foot of the sail so that, when the boat luffs, the forward part of the sail lifts at the same time at the head and the foot. Of course, to see this properly you need woollen tell-tales at several points along the luff. With the mainsail things are more difficult, because for the lower two-thirds the effect of the wind coming off the jib must be taken into account. The mainsail therefore needs twist, and it is the amount of twist that is important. This can best be assessed with tell-tales as well, and control is with the kicking strap: more tension for less twist.

A new sail shape without the usual aerofoil section is beginning to make its mark internationally. As the sail comes off the mast the shape is very similar to a standard sail, but then it goes into a flattened section, curving again only in the batten area. This type of sail was first seen on the Twelve Metres in the America's Cup trials in 1974 and was dubbed the 'Frisbee Cut'. Originating in the NASA laboratories it has yet to prove itself markedly superior, although it seems a good base for experiments.

The quickest way to ensure boatspeed is to calibrate all the moving controls, then sail the boat in a race and record all the settings. The important ones are shroud tensions, mast bend, outhaul, kicking strap, mainsheet slider, mainsheet, jib halyard, jib sheet, sheet leads, forestay, backstay, sails, crew weight, mean wind speed, air temperature, size of waves and performance. After several races a pattern will emerge and daily guesswork will be eliminated. Air temperature is very important, for the colder the weather the denser the wind; this winter tuning for a major series in the summer can be very misleading. I realized this many years ago in an ocean racer on a trip back from Deauville when in 26 to 28 knots of breeze on a cold early spring day we were down to no. 4 jib and two reefs in the main. Later in the year in the same strength of wind from the same direction we were able to carry full sail because the weather was warmer.

The most important factor for boatspeed is that the boat should be perfectly balanced. This has been the case in all the fast boats that I have had, and I try to go out with a new boat in Force 3 to 4 winds and adjust the rig until it sails to windward with virtually negative helm. I note the settings and then, as the wind increases or decreases, I adjust the rig so that the helm remains the same. On a windward leg I estimate that some adjustment to the rig is needed every fifteen seconds, thus getting the balance right is my number one priority for boatspeed.

Laser

Ian Bruce

Chapter 6

Canadian Olympic representative *Finn* 1960, *Star* 1972; Prince of Wales Cup winner 1967 and 1968. Managing Director of Performance Sailcraft, the world-wide *Laser* builders.

The *Laser* is the most successful boat of the 1970s. A growth rate of over ten thousand a year has ensured for this single-hander a place in yachting history. It was designed by Bruce Kirby, who had previously produced some top International 14 designs, though it was as much the efforts of the builders that brought the *Laser* its success. They insisted on the no-compromise one-design concept. This effectively gave everyone the same chance of winning; what counted was sailing ability and attention to detail rather than a bottomless purse. This has meant that there is great attention to detail among the top *Laser* sailors and has proved that there is no substitute for 'sailing time' when it comes to success.

Length: 4230 mm
Beam: 1370 mm
Sailarea: 7·06 sq m
Weight: 68·04 kg

Since the *Laser* is the sort of beast it is, a totally one-design concept, the hull, centreboard and rudder are not very important factors in boatspeed. Boatspeed is all a matter of the rig and, in order of importance, the things that

Harry Jemmett (Canada) at the Laser World Championship in Bermuda, 1974.

matter are the outhaul, mainsheet tension, cunningham and kicking strap. Each of these is almost as important as steering the boat properly in flat water, though it is in a seaway that steering comes into its own. I have tabulated the controls on a *Laser* and how they should be set for all conditions.

The hull must be looked after, however: it is no use attempting to win races with a neglected boat. It must be clean, which is pretty easy, and should be highly polished with a good hard wax polish of the type used for cars. I don't believe in having a wet sanded surface, in an attempt to induce laminar flow for a greater distance along the hull. Even if this is possible, it makes little sense when balancing the forces of a boat smashing up and down in waves against the skill of proper steering. Downwind, the wet sanded surface has a distinct disadvantage: it tends to carry more water 'attached' to the boat at a time when you are trying to skid over the water as much as possible. Nor is a rubbed-down surface conducive to 'breaking away', unlike a polished one.

The centreboard of the *Laser* should be well rubbed down everywhere except close to the leading edge. The centreboard is carefully shaped to a NACA 0009 section, which is a 'turbulent flow' section. Roughness close to the leading edge acts as a

Wind	Sailing Angle	Sail Camber	Outhaul	Cunningham	Kicker (Vang)	Traveller	Mainsheet
1. Very light/drift	Very free	Flat as possible	Tight enough so foot of sail touches boom without horizontal fold	None	Tight enough to bend mast	Right off	No tension. Boom should be well out past corner of transom
2. Light (flat water)	Close as possible	Flat	As in 1, but wind will stretch sail *just* away from boom	Just enough to remove diagonal wrinkles	Little less than 1. Allow a little twist	Just enough to keep blocks apart	Little tension; pull from boom pulley to centre boom
3. Light (leftover chop)	Free	Little fuller than 2	Ease sail about 3 inches from boom	Leave hint of diagonal wrinkles	As in 1	As in 2	Boom further outboard almost to corner of transom. Sail free
4. Medium (flat water)	Close as possible	Full	Tighten till foot touches boom	Remove wrinkles	Not used upwind. Set for reach	4 inches off deck	Moderate tension. Boom close to centreline (6–8 inches)
5. Medium (chop)	Slightly free	Very full	Ease 2–3 inches away from boom	Leave hint of wrinkles	As in 4	Tight to deck	Moderate tension but boom at end of traveller run
6. Strong (flat water or long wave pattern)	Close	Very flat	Tight as possible	Maximum tension; pull beyond point that wrinkles disappear	Very tight (to hold down boom when sheet eased in puffs)	Tight to deck	Maximum tension. Boom at end of traveller run
7. Strong (chop)	Free	Fuller than 6	Ease sail 1–2 inches off boom	As in 6	As in 6	Ease till block 3–4 inches above deck	Pull boom inboard 3–4 inches on traveller and ease sheet slightly to twist upper sail

turbulator. The flow over this section can be upset by making the entry too smooth, and performance improves noticeably with a roughish entry in light weather.

The rudder is similar to the centreboard and should be treated in the same way. It is sufficiently strong, but watch the pivot bolt carefully to ensure that there is no play between the cheeks and the blade. It also pays to have a tight-fitting tiller in the rudder head.

There must be no play in the connection between the upper and lower mast sections, otherwise a hard spot will be induced in the bend and this will wreck the set of the sail, causing a girt from the clew to the luff at the join of the mast.

Nothing can be done about the cut of a *Laser* sail, for they are all as alike as it is possible to make them, being computer-cut to a master pattern. It is important, however, to understand how the sail is cut. The luff is a combination of seam curving, which is sewn in shape, and a fairly large luff curve, that is, extra cloth beyond the straight line from the head to the tack. When the mast is fully bent by mainsheet tension, the luff round does not contribute any camber or shape to the sail, but when the mast straightens this extra cloth becomes an important part of the sail's shape. This is not a problem in strong

breezes; to windward the sail is fairly flat and the pressure of the wind opens up the leech. Downwind, the mast straightens up and the sail becomes fuller for more efficient reaching.

In light winds, and particularly in drifting conditions, the *Laser* sailor is faced with a problem. The extra cloth of the luff round lies in the area of the sail close to the mast and produces an undesirable section in the sail. This section is such that the sail comes away from the mast almost at right angles to the centreline of the boat and curves quickly into a totally flat sail, right out to the leech. The wind does not have enough energy to push the extra cloth back into the sail to form a regular, continuous curved section, and so the only way to smooth out the sail is to bend the mast, which over-flattens the sail, however.

Nor does the problem stop here. By bending the mast with the mainsheet in light weather, the leech is over-tightened and hooks to windward. The boom must therefore be sheeted wide, and the only way to get the sail to set properly is to use the kicking strap to control the mast bend. Then the sail camber will be correct, and the mainsheet is used only to control the athwartships position of the boom without imparting any vertical tension. It is all too easy, however, to make the mistake of having a sail that is too full in

Length: 4230 mm
Beam: 1370 mm
Sailarea: 7·06 sq m
Weight: 68·04 kg

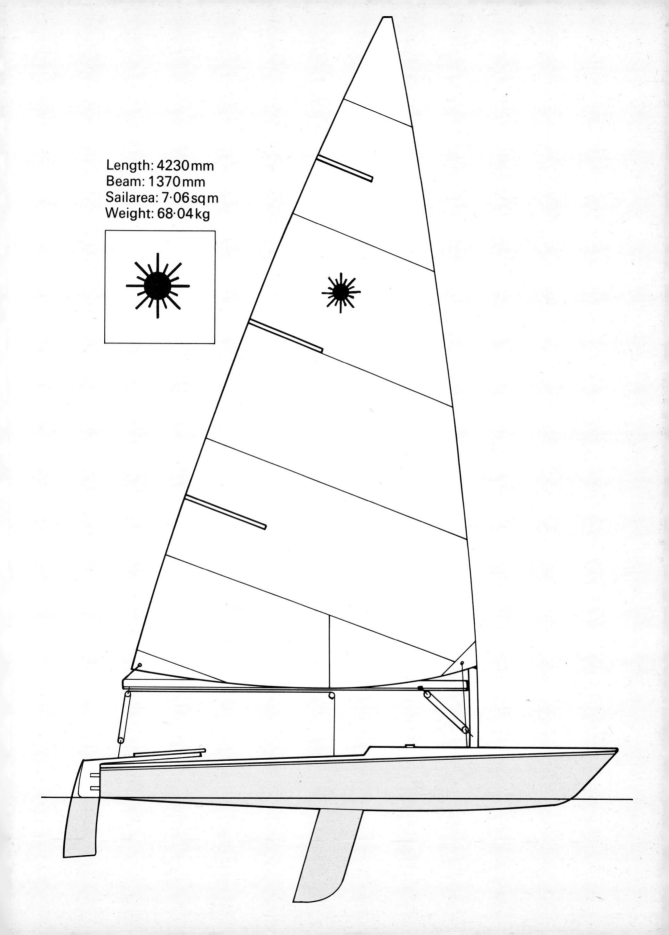

very light winds. In general, the sail on the *Laser* can be flatter than most people think it should be, at least for upwind sailing.

The mainsail outhaul makes a tremendous difference to the camber of the sail. I find it helpful to think of the sail as a club-footed genoa and the outhaul as the positioning of the sheet lead. If the lead is moved too far forward it makes the sail too full with a tight leech. Then it is both inefficient and hard to hold upright. If the sheet lead is too far aft the sail can be made too flat and the leech too open, thus taking drive out of the sail.

The table shows the best positions for the various controls of the *Laser* for upwind sailing in most wind and wave conditions.

A few modifications can be made to the *Laser* to achieve greater efficiency. It is well worth padding the toe-strap with thick neoprene tubing – this makes sitting out much more comfortable. It is also a good idea to rig the clew outhaul as a 3:1 tackle as shown in the diagram (for reasons of clarity the short rope strop which holds the clew down on to the boom has been omitted). This enables the outhaul to be moved whilst sailing upwind. Similarly,

it is simple to rig the cunningham control as a 6:1 tackle by incorporating a loop knot into the first part of the downhaul and using this as a fairlead, as shown in the diagram.

For the mainsheet there should be a well-positioned, fast-release yet positive cam cleat on each side deck. These cleats should be raised off the deck so that knuckles don't get scraped across the non-slip surface of the deck. Used with or without a ratchet block, this system is definitely preferable to the centre-swivel cam cleat as the sheet cannot be cleated and uncleated fast enough with the centre jammer. It is extremely important, especially for lighter people, that the mainsheet is constantly worked in a breeze.

Up to a point, the *Laser* is a forgiving boat. It also rewards the good sailor, one who is prepared to practise in all weathers. It is highly responsive to sail trim, which must be thoroughly understood in order to achieve maximum efficiency from the rig.

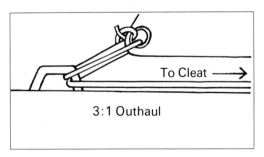

3:1 Outhaul

To Cleat →

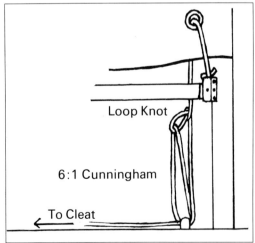

Loop Knot

6:1 Cunningham

To Cleat ←

Wendy Fitzpatrick, the first British Laser Champion,
adequately demonstrates the requisites for success – a
feel for the boat and eyes on the sail. Note the extra
extension on the tiller, a piece of rope. This can only be
used because of the Laser's inherent weather helm,
and then only to windward.

Finn

John Maynard

Chapter 7

British Olympic representative in Finns, 1968; Finn National Champion, 1966 and 1968. Olympic coach for Britain.

After the 1948 Olympic Games, when the *Firefly* had been sailed in the singlehanded class, it was agreed that a new class designed specifically for single-handed sailing was needed. The winner of the competitive trials was the *Finn,* designed by Rickard Sarby of Finland. It was first sailed in the Olympics at Helsinki in 1952, when Paul Elvström won his second Gold Medal, and has appeared ever since. By modern standards it is a heavy boat, yet it has developed through the skills and ingenuity of the people who sail it. The unstayed cantilever rig has now become highly sophisticated, and the transition from wooden spars to metal ones came before the Kiel Olympics. The dispute about the merits of glassfibre and wooden hulls continues, though the double-bottomed glass boats are beginning to find favour among the top helmsmen.

Length: 4500mm
Beam: 1510mm (maximum)
Sailarea: 10sqm
Weight: 145kg (minimum)

It is very difficult to distinguish the importance of different aspects of boat-tuning. In the *Finn* class, however, it is easy to purchase a fast hull off the shelf;

Chris Law (K 321) at pre-Olympic CORK 1975.

the only problem then is to fit it out so that everything works properly and efficiently. Nothing can be done with the centreplate as it is cut out of sheet aluminium, although the thicker it is the better (8 to 10mm optimum). Nor is the rudder critical, so long as it is well finished and aerodynamically sectioned. What is important is the rig.

The mast is unstayed and the way in which it bends both sideways and fore and aft is very important. Since metal masts were introduced manufacturers have learnt to reproduce the required bend characteristics time and time again, a far cry from the days spent planing wooden ones and then gluing more wood back when they became too limber. Booms are now easy to obtain, too, and emphasis has shifted to sails.

Most of the development in *Finns* is centred around the sail, and it is no coincidence that most of the top international *Finn* sailors work very closely with their sailmakers. Sails are now becoming more standardized so that what counts is the quality of the helmsman and his boat-handling abilities, tactics, fitness and mental approach.

The *Finn* hull must be of minimum weight and as stiff as possible. Considering the relatively high all-up weight it is not difficult to get it stiff. The centreboard case must be held rigidly in the hull, preferably with deep and wide knees. Since the introduction of the pendulum method of measuring the weight distribution in *Finns*, the ends have become considerably lighter. Transoms are thinner, and decks too, so that more material can be used to make the bottom of the hull stiff.

The hull must be fair and, so far as glassfibre hulls are concerned, this entirely depends on the boat-builder. Little can be done with small bumps and hollows, but the larger ones should either be filled with plastic putty or rubbed out with wet-and-dry sandpaper. Glass boats have a tendency to develop hollows when they are left resting on trailer pads for long periods. The answer is to support the hull over as large an area as possible; as much of the weight as possible should be supported on the hog, not on the skin. Wooden boats need constant attention, since different parts of the wood 'move' at different rates because of their varying water soakage rates. High spots can be removed with a very sharp plane and hollows filled with plastic putty. All wooden boats should have at least eight to ten coats of two-part polyurethane paint or varnish on both sides to keep out as much of the moisture as possible. If it feels smooth the finish is adequate.

Tolerances of 5 mm do not allow much change of shape in the hull, but even within these limits significant boatspeed differences do occur. The hull should be maximum length, narrow along the waterline and widening at the transom. The waterline entry should be straight and the run aft flat. It is doubtful whether the double bottom that is now allowed brings any real benefit; it is difficult to keep it watertight and impossible to see if any water is trapped in it.

The anodized aluminium alloy centreboard needs little attention. Wipe it occasionally with fresh warm water and a cloth sprinkled with abrasive cleaning powder. Solid mahogany rudders are still in use, though very good fibreglass foam filled ones have now come on the market. The rudder must be stiff and fair and have an aerodynamic section with the maximum chord about one-third of the way aft, a rounded leading edge and a fine trailing edge.

The shape of the boom is closely controlled by the class rules. It should be stiff both longitudinally and laterally, even if this means that it is slightly heavier than the minimum weight.

The mast must be of minimum weight with its centre of gravity as low as possible. Since it is unstayed it will bend under the action of aerodynamic forces, of the mainsheet via the leech of the sail and of shock forces when

Length: 4500 mm
Beam: 1510 mm (maximum)
Sailarea: 10 sqm
Weight: 145 kg (minimum)

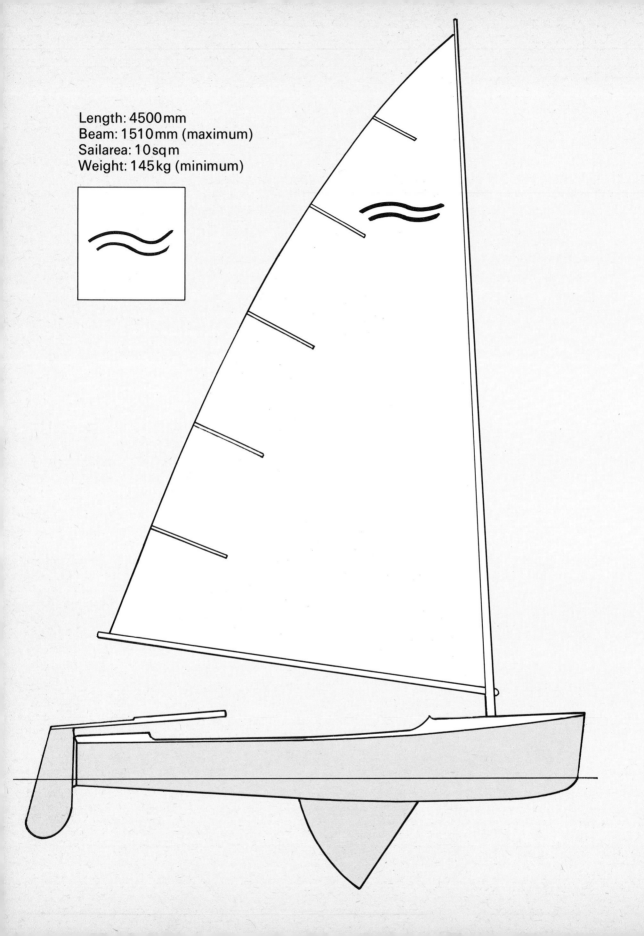

slamming through waves. The faster ones have an even curve with no sudden bends or kinks and a lot of curve low down. The middle section should scarcely bend sideways. This is essential for good pointing. As the wind freshens, however, the top 4 feet of the mast must fall off sideways a little to assist the leech to open, or else the helmsman will begin to be overpowered. The stronger the wind the more this sideways fall-off must be. Sideways flexibility is highly critical for performance: too much too soon and pointing ability is lost with the leech freed; not enough means that the helmsman is struggling and the boat overpowered.

The *Finn* masts made today are stiffer in the head than earlier examples, and this has led to a slightly heavier breed of *Finn* sailors. The mast must flex sideways a little, low down, to absorb the shock effects when going through waves, so as to stop the rig from stalling as the boat slows down; otherwise it is difficult to steer.

The mast must be of the minimum diameter consistent with producing the correct fore and aft and sideways bending. It is here that the metal mast really scores over the old wooden ones, the reduced diameter bringing less drag and therefore better pointing. Metal masts can be made to guaranteed bend characteristics and this in turn helps the sailmaker to design the best sail. Higher tensile strength and lack of flaws in alloy masts mean that a far higher degree of low-down bending can be obtained without fear of breakage. Masts are set more upright to give a better downwind performance, more clearance under the boom when tacking or gybing; yet the mast can still be raked back, by bending, for windward work.

This new tuning of the rig means that sails have to be cut with either a great deal of luff round or broad seaming, to accommodate the bend in the mast. With the mast bent the sails are fairly flat, though there is considerable leech tension. Even so the top of the sail is designed to twist off in fresh winds. Because of the higher leech tensions, the mainsheet traveller is set further outboard. Control of sail shape is a big factor in boatspeed. The design of the sail is important, though the helmsman's sail control is what really counts. Upwind, three controls are necessary, each of which must be to hand on each side of the boat. The mast bend is controlled through the mainsheet. The cunningham can flatten the sail and move the draft forward, tidy up the wrinkles and open the leech. The clew outhaul also helps to control the leech; if it is let in, the leech will hook to windward in the lower part and help the pointing ability. Pulling the foot out

opens the bottom of the leech and increases footing power.

In 5- to 10-knot winds, it is important to have the leech standing up straight with very little twist in the sail. The cunningham eye should be eased, as should the clew outhaul. The boom should be eased off the deck a couple of inches to increase the flow in the sail, but not so much that it starts to twist. In lighter winds, with the helmsman off the side deck, the *Finn* rig becomes very inefficient. At these times the helmsman should encourage the sail to twist by letting the boom lift up. This straightens the mast and makes the sail very full with the draft well forward, though this is not good for pointing. The leech can never twist off freely because of the weight of the long *Finn* boom pulling down on it. The *Finn* will not go well in light weather with any applied leech tension, so the only solution is to let everything off, except the clew outhaul which should be pulled out to unhook the leech, sheet the boom well out on the traveller and sit in the bottom of the boat and relax!

In heavy winds the cunningham eye should be pulled down hard and the clew pulled right out. The boom should

John Maynard is broad reaching his Finn on Grafham Water – note the completely neutral helm, a sign of a boat perfectly balanced.

then be sheeted well down, so that the end just touches the deck and is set well out on the traveller. The sail should then be as flat as possible and will twist off at the top to reduce the side force. In very heavy winds, especially in the slams, the mainsheet traveller runs out and the mainsheet has to be eased to let the boom go out further and increase sail twist. At this stage the *Finn* is almost on a close reach.

Downwind sail shape is controlled by the kicking strap. It is easy to find the best position for average wind strengths by determining just how much you can carry, easing the kicker to reduce power. In very heavy winds, where survival is everything, on the broad reaches and runs, the kicker should be let well off. The resultant helm imbalance caused by the excessive sail twist must be corrected by sheeting the boom well in. This helps to reduce the massive forces on the sail and also cocks the boom up so that it is less likely to dig in if the boat develops a roll. It is advisable to have the plate two-thirds down in these conditions.

In winds below 8 knots, on a run, especially in a sloppy sea, it again pays to let the kicker off and let the boom out beyond the square position. This seems to encourage air flow across the sail and gives a little more speed. At the same time the boat is heeled to windward with the helmsman's weight well forward.

It is important to keep the gear simple. Some systems are essential, however. The kicking strap must be adjustable underway, most simply with a lever. The angle of the kicking strap to the boom is poor because of the proximity of the boom to the deck, but the strap is more effective if the attachment point is well back along the boom. Heavy-gauge stainless steel wire is necessary to avoid stretch and possible breakages because the tension on the poorly-angled strap is enormous.

The J.C. strap is a heavy duty shockcord attached halfway along the boom; it passes through a block on the stem of the boat and then back around the other side of the mast to the boom. It is kept under considerable tension and has the effect of pulling the boom out to leeward. This holds the boom steady when reaching or running in sloppy seas with a light wind. It enables the boat to be sailed heeled to windward without the boom falling back to the middle of the boat. It gives more rapid trimming and speeds the gybe in light to moderate winds. It is now a vital piece of equipment.

Tall helmsmen tend to sit out with their heels close to the floor at all times. Shorter skippers have to adjust their toe-straps according to the conditions, letting them come up in a blow and pulling them downwards in lighter winds. A control line to the straps is arranged so that it can be adjusted whilst sitting out, but it must have a knot in it just in case the skipper fails to cleat it!

Tempest

Alan Warren

Chapter 8

Olympic Silver Medallist 1972; three times British Open Champion; four times Merlin-Rocket National Champion.

The *Tempest* was chosen as an International class after the prototype had performed at a series of selection trials in Holland in 1965; it completely dominated the racing and was the overwhelming first choice. As a class it grew sufficiently to take its place at the Olympic Games at Kiel in 1972, where twenty-one nations were represented. It is totally one-design, and licensed builders construct the boats from a master set of moulds. It is not a dinghy with a keel stuck on, a criticism often levelled at it, but a boat in the mainstream of design aimed at a lighter, faster and more responsive craft.

Length: 6680 mm
Beam: 1880 mm
Sailarea: 22·92 sq m (main and jib), 20·9 sq m (spinnaker)
Weight: 444 kg

The class rules ensure that the construction of the *Tempest* is tightly and carefully controlled. The class is specifically designed for glassfibre reinforced plastics construction, and certain materials are banned – among them Kevlar and epoxy resin. Thus all the hulls are very much alike. The better builders do try to get the boats right and

At the gybe mark in the final race at CORK 1974.

to make sure that there is no shrinkage of the hull between the reinforcing frames. If such shrinkage is bad, the outside of the hull looks like the rib cage of an emaciated horse and the boat is useless. The lines of a *Tempest* are slacker than those of a centreboarder and it is imperative that they are kept fair. Any depressions must be filled in with a french chalk and resin mixture, and the whole area rubbed smooth using a large pad behind the glasspaper so that the hollows do not recur.

I consider that hull finish is one of the most important factors in good boatspeed in this class. It takes a long time and a lot of hard work to get a good finish, but it is worthwhile in the end. Once the hull has been faired it must be progressively polished with finer grades of glasspaper and finished with car bodywork rubbing compound.

In one area in particular the hull must be tremendously stiff – around the shroud anchorages. If the hull is at all weak at these points there will be heavy distortion as the loads imposed on the *Tempest* here are higher than those on a centreboard boat. The stability afforded by the keel multiplies the strains. It is in this area, too, that the jib is sheeted, further complicating the loading. It therefore pays to tie the jib sheet fairlead to both the gunwale and the mast partners using aluminium tube or angle. The integral support provided in the construction of the hull should be capable of withstanding all the strains, though after a time the fibreglass will begin to delaminate; the aluminium supports will help to delay this process considerably.

The *Tempest* keel is made of steel plate with a lead bulb. It was designed so that it could be lifted up into the hull with only the bulb protruding, thus giving ease of trailing. This, however, brought other problems: if the keel is slung this way it will vibrate in the case and slow the boat considerably. To be competitive the *Tempest* must have its keel rigidly fixed in the box. The steel plate part of the keel which is in the box in the hull must be carefully packed and the bottom of the box sealed. The keel must be packed so it can be taken out for measurement at the major regattas. Tufnol strips of equal thickness on each side should be glued and screwed to the keel along the line of the bottom of the box so that the Tufnol forms a smooth fairing with the bottom of the boat. Two other strips should also be glued and screwed to the keel at the top of the plate box. Strips downwards are unnecessary as they will only lie against the weak, unsupported plate box sides. With these four Tufnol strips in place the keel should be easily removed, though only with some effort; any chance that the keel might move while the boat is underway will be eliminated

by tightening the retaining bolts on top of the plate box. To finish the job properly the slight gaps in the bottom of the box should be filled in, large gaps at the ends with a mixture of french chalk and resin, though around the area where the plate moves a non-hardening filler must be used.

The keel itself must be looked after. Any depressions must be filled and the whole thing rubbed smooth. Coat it with plenty of paint, rubbing down well between each coat with waterproof glasspaper, getting the final finish with car-burnishing compound. Hard, two-pack polyurethane paint is the best for the keel; that and a whole lot of hard work!

The rudder can be made either of glassfibre or of wood. The one I use I have made from plywood so that it is as light as possible. It has to conform to the profile limits of the class, though the section is free. I prefer an aerofoil section with a parabolic entry with the maximum chord back to nearly 50 per cent and the trailing edge very sharp. The most important thing to remember about the rudder is that the curve of the section must be the same on both sides to stop vibration. Once again the finish is all important, and I treat it in the same way as the keel. The rudder unit has to be removable, but there is no reason why the standard heavy framework should be retained. All that is required is a strip of wood top and bottom to fair in the hull and to support the central pivot; the rest can be filled with expanded polystyrene.

I try to keep the decks as uncluttered as possible, particularly the foredeck, so as to cut down the windage to the bare minimum. Any disturbed flow of air reduces the efficiency potential of the rig. Most of my rivals do not seem to pay enough attention to the effect of windage on their boats, their rigs and themselves. Loose clothing, for instance, causes drag, and when you are trying to win races you want everything going for you.

The most important fact about the mast is that it should be strong enough to do the job in all weathers. It must, however, be as light as possible and have as small a section as the class rules allow. To keep the windage factor down, I like to rig the mast simply. The fashion for a standing backstay with a rig which also has a pair of diamond wires is unnecessarily complicated in my opinion. The diamond wire on the leeward side goes slack and vibrates, disturbing the air flow in the slot, the most important area to keep free from disturbance. The backstay is invariably slack when going to windward, and this vibrates too, causing drag. Both are unnecessary with a simple rig using swept-back aerofoil spreaders fixed at the mast. With these there is greater

control of the shape of the mast and far less need to use the mast ram at the partners.

Shroud adjustments underway I do find useful, but only to a limited degree. With easily adjustable shrouds it is simple to set up one's rig for the existing conditions; we rake the mast further aft as the wind blows harder. With the forestay adjustable and fixed spreaders there is no limit to control of the shape of the mast.

The boom must be as light as possible and as stiff as it can be made. The mainsheet take-off points should be easy to adjust fore and aft as the pressure on the gooseneck helps to induce, or control, the bend of the mast. The outhaul must be led from the forward end of the boom to each side of the boat for ease of control. The boom must be strong as a powerful kicking-strap system incorporating a lever is essential to control the leech tension of the large mainsail.

The spinnaker contributes much to the speed of the *Tempest*, particularly in surfing conditions. The class allows spinnaker chutes but people are reluctant to have them fitted as it means moving the forestay and jib tack back a little, thereby closing the slot between the jib and the mainsail. If the system used is thoroughly understood by the crew, so much so that the kite can be hoisted and lowered blindfold, then

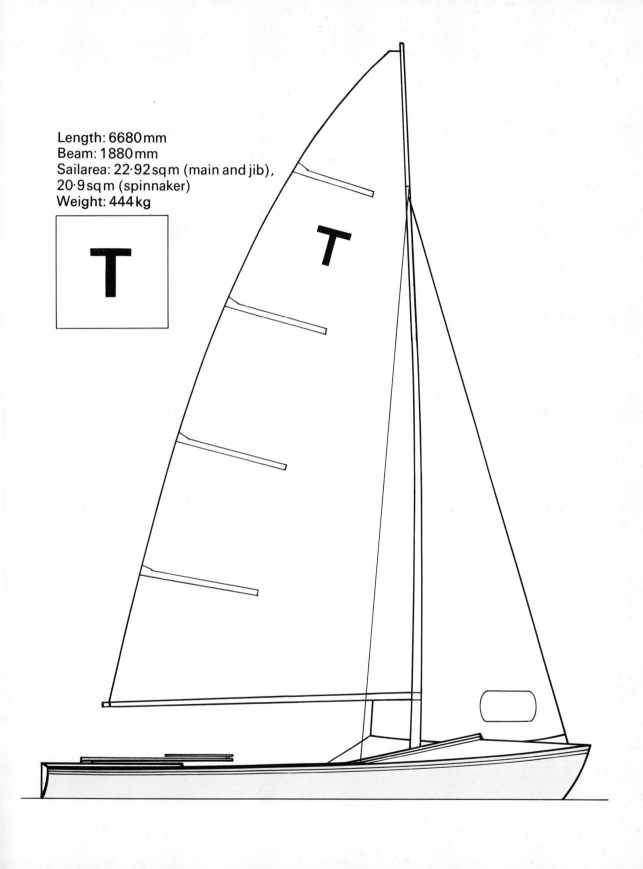

Length: 6680 mm
Beam: 1880 mm
Sailarea: 22·92 sq m (main and jib),
20·9 sq m (spinnaker)
Weight: 444 kg

T

there is nothing wrong with it. It must therefore be kept simple. The boom must be as stiff and light as possible and a simple wire and hook vang system into an eye on the boom is best. One further disadvantage of the spinnaker chute is that a lot of water can be trapped in it, thus adding to the weight of the boat where you least want weight.

Sails seem a mystery to me. Cuts vary according to the cloth and their shapes. I like to know that mine are full sized and that when they are up they look right. If you don't think they look right, then it's ten to one they won't go. Of course the shape can be altered underway and the relationship of the mainsail and the jib is most important. The jib leech tension has much to do with this and it is worth spending some

time before the start making sure that it not only looks right but feels right, too. If it is too tight the boat slows because of the backwind effect on the mainsail and if it is too slack the boat will not point. If the luff of the mainsail lifts too much, then the jib leech is too tight; to check that it is not too slack measure the tacking angle with the compasses.

Preparation of the boat is most important and must be kept simple so that afloat you can devote your energies to sailing it as fast as possible. There is no use having a nagging worry about the set-up when you are trying to get the best from the wind and picking your way carefully through the waves or are looking for the big helpful wave on the reaching and running legs. Sailing the boat must be second nature, and there is no substitute for practice.

Soon after the start of the final race at CORK 1974, the white-hulled boat to windward of US 217 has tacked to go to the favoured side of the course; US 217 wants to tack but is obviously doubtful as to whether he can cross G 135.

470

Phil Crebbin

Chapter 9

British National and Open Champion, 1975; Enterprise World and National Champion, 1974; Albacore National Champion, 1974; runner-up Albacore World Championship, 1973; Endeavour Trophy winner, 1974 and 1975.

The *470* class was designed in France by André Cornu, initially for domestic racing only. It spread slowly even after it was granted full international status by the IYRU. Its selection in 1972 as an Olympic class for 1976 gave it great impetus, although there were already ten thousand *470s* in existence. The French-dominated class committee has to some extent stifled its growth by imposing unusual building standards inconsistent with the development of boatbuilding techniques. It has, however, ensured a one-design class, though at the price of a boat which is difficult to maintain at the top limits of competition for any great period.

Length: 4700 mm
Beam: 1720 mm
Sailarea: 13·29 sq m (main and jib), 13·01 sq m (spinnaker)
Weight: 118 kg (minimum)

No one single factor produces fantastic boatspeed, rather a combination of many. Since all things are equal in most *470s*, it is the rig that provides the greatest scope for improving speed. Unfortunately it is not

David White close spinnaker reaching at the German Open Championship, 1975.

a matter of one mast or one suit of sails being best, but rather the way that the two match or are made to match by the way the rig is set up. The rig has a large number of variables, each of which can be controlled. Unless the helmsman knows exactly what each control does and when to use it, littering boats with alleged 'go-fasts' is bad practice; it is far better to keep it simple. However, it is ability to use all the fine controls that produces that extra amount of boatspeed necessary to take you to the front and keep you there.

Mast and boom stiffness, both sideways and fore and aft; sail camber and the position of maximum flow; amount of luff round; jib luff tension; jib sheeting angle; jib leech tension; mainsail luff and foot tensions; batten stiffness and tension; kicking strap and mainsheet tensions; traveller position; mast bend; spreader length and angle; all are variable. Getting all of them right is the secret of success in the *470*, but what suits one man may not be right even for a boat with identical crew weight, because the limits imposed in the class mean that there is a difference in the way a boat is set up for each particular helmsman's style of sailing.

All the *470* builders aim to produce a fast hull. Most important is that it should have the minimum all-up weight, be stiff, and that the moment of inertia should be as low as possible.

Slight variations in hull shape have not made any significant difference in boatspeed, although everyone seems to have their ideal hull shape. The *470* hull does not cut through waves, instead it bounces over them. Consequently, if the hull is soft, some power from the rig will be absorbed by the hull flexing as it meets the waves. The stiffer the hull, the more of the rig's power will be directed to driving the boat forwards. To make the boat pitch as little as possible in these conditions, the moment of inertia in the pitching plane should be made as low as possible by concentrating as much of the weight of the hull as possible into the middle of the boat, with the greatest concentration under the mast; the amounts of glass cloth used in the hull laminate should tail off towards the bow and stern.

Centreboards and rudders are very important in the *470* as the rules do not allow any alteration from a flat board except over a limited distance from each edge. For a high-performance dinghy this makes the leading-edge shape highly critical if one is to avoid aeration and stalling in heavy weather. Aim for a parabolic entry, not too blunt and with no hard points where the fairing-in meets the flat part of the board. The trailing edge should taper gradually until it leaves a squared-off back end $\frac{1}{8}$th of an inch thick; again no hard spots where the fairing-in meets the flat part

of the board. Where the rudder blade goes into the water it helps to sharpen the leading edge to a point over about 2 inches in order to reduce the amount of air sucked down, thus minimizing any tendency to stall. Stalling is more likely to occur in a badly-sailed boat; if the boat is in perfect balance, there is hardly any chance of stalling the rudder.

The centreboard and rudder should be firmly fixed so that they do not rock – another certain way of stalling is to allow movement in either of them. The class rules permit packing strips to be fitted inside the centreboard case as long as they go the full length; they must be fitted so that the board, when fully down, fits tightly between them. Gybing boards are not allowed on the *470* although some helmsmen try to produce the same effect by allowing the board to rake forward when it is fully down. This has dubious value, but it is essential for the board to go down until the leading edge makes a 90-degree angle with the waterline of the boat. The fit of the rudder blade in the stock of the lifting rudder must be tight, as must the fit of the tiller to the rudder stock. Just how far the blade goes down depends on personal preference. I have it vertical so that the helm is as light as possible. In light weather on flat water I sometimes raise the blade a small amount. Both centreboards and rudders should be as stiff as possible

Length: 4700mm
Beam: 1720mm
Sailarea: 13·29sqm (main and jib),
13·01sqm (spinnaker)
Weight: 118kg (minimum)

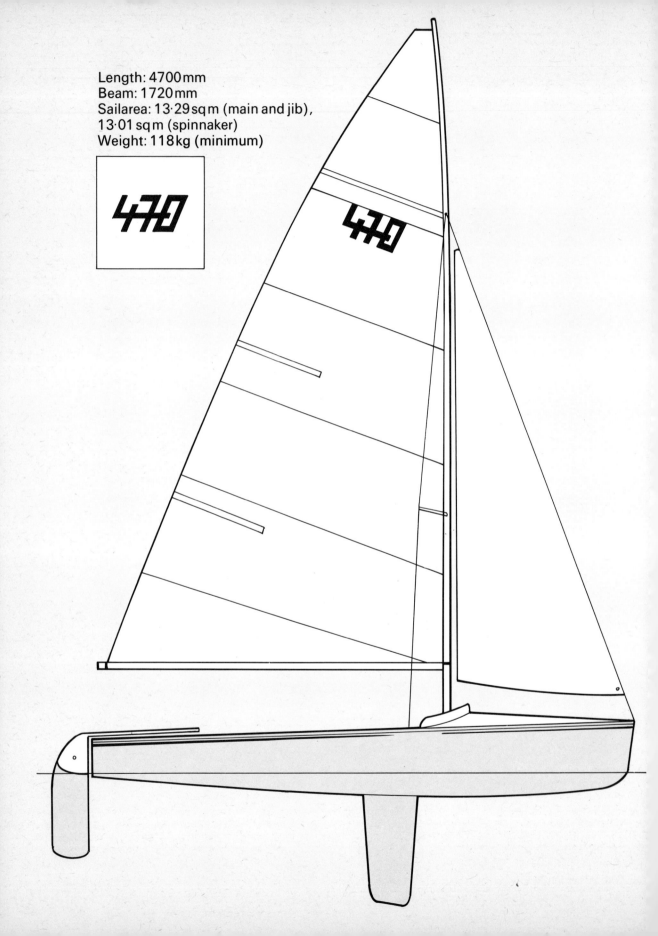

but not over heavy. Mine are made of 1-inch wide laminates, of mahogany and spruce alternately, running up and down the boards and are light and very stiff.

The *470* rig has two main problems. Only one set of sails and spars is permitted at any regatta, and the optimum rig varies considerably for different conditions. In light weather it pays to have a flat mainsail set up with considerable twist; in medium to heavy weather a full sail with a fairly tight leech is required to give the boat 'drive', particularly in a choppy sea; in progressively heavier weather, according to crew weight, the sail must be flattened again with the leech open at the head. The jib must complement the mainsail at all times. If you start with a flat sail on a straight mast, there is no way of inducing fullness in medium weather. Likewise, with a full sail for medium airs, the boat will be sluggish in light airs without extreme mast bend; it is useless to bend the mast with mainsheet and kicker tensions only as this will produce a tight leech, which is not wanted.

Setting the mast with the correct bend for light weather is not easy in a *470*, for the powerful deck rams allowed in other classes are banned. The only way of doing it is by raking the spreaders aft of the straight line from the hounds to the shrouds, so that

when the jib halyard is tightened the mast is forced forward by the spreaders and a bend induced. Once that bend is started, compression will do the rest. The mainsail can then be cut to fit the bend and the sail used in light weather with twist, because the mast bend is not caused either by mainsheet or by kicker tension. In medium winds putting a chock in front of the mast at the deck will prevent it bending quite so much.

The problem of getting a sail to fit this set-up lies with the sailmaker. It is a tricky business, because if all the mast bend is catered for in the luff round, straightening the mast will create a sail with too full an entry. Conversely, if all the fullness in the sail comes from the seams, mast bend will create nasty creases, particularly from the clew to the inboard end of the bottom batten and especially when bending the mast in a blow.

If a rig of this type is to work effectively, the mast must be fairly flexible so that it bends readily under jib halyard tension. At least an 8:1 purchase is needed on the jib halyard, and if this is fitted on to a 2:1 whip, so that 16:1 power is developed, all the better. Bend low down is best, as this has the greatest effect on the part of the sail with most fullness and where it is used most effectively; that is, in the slot area. Sideways bend is controlled by the length of the spreaders; the longer

the spreaders the stiffer the mast, sideways. Fore and aft bend can be increased by sawing through the luff groove part of the mast above the hounds. This helps the mast to bend and twist off the top of the sail, opening the leech of the mainsail.

The boom should be as stiff as possible because if it flexes it will not allow good control of the leech tension of the mainsail. Hardening the kicking strap only bends the boom; it does not tighten the leech.

As only one spinnaker is carried, it must be a compromise, halfway between a full sail for running and a flat one for reaching. On a true Olympic course with a 90-degree angle at the gybe mark, the reaches are fairly broad so that the spinnaker tends to be cut on the fuller side of flat; but with fixed-length reaches the broad-shouldered sail will be shorter in the height of the middle seam than a more narrow-shouldered sail. A lot of different shapes can be found at the front of the fleet.

The spinnaker boom must be light and stiff. Perhaps more important, the end fittings must work properly at all times; most manufacturers' fittings need slight doctoring and constant attention. The best vang system is one

At the gybe mark, pre-Olympic CORK 1975.

made of wire which connects to an eye on the pole with a hook.

A functional layout with the fewest possible loose ends is most important. Free running blocks and wire help, and the kicking strap and the cunningham controls should be led to each side of the boat. I use a 4:1 purchase on top of a lever for the kicker, giving a purchase of 24:1. For the cunningham 4:1 is quite adequate and I like to have a light shockcord to pull the sail back up in light weather. For the centreboard I use a continuous 3:1 tackle that allows me to adjust the centreboard height while sailing. If the board is a snug fit it will not twist and jam. One other refinement which can only be used in a boat without a spinnaker chute is a 1:2 spinnaker halyard; this makes the job of hoisting that much quicker.

Whatever happens, avoid complicated fittings for, if you cannot use them, they are so much useless weight in the boat. If anything moves it must be calibrated and a record of the settings kept so that a pattern can be established. One of the things that makes a top sailor is his ability to pinpoint the reasons for every good or bad performance.

Tornado

Reg White

Chapter 10

European Tornado Champion 1973, twice runner-up; four times runner-up in Tornado World Championships, and winner, 1976; winner, Little America's Cup 1963, 1964, 1965, 1966 and 1968. Boatbuilder.

The *Tornado* was designed by Rodney March for the IYRU two-man catamaran trials in 1967. Built within the B division limits, she dominated the trials and was selected as the new class for international racing. The class became immediately popular, as much because of the boat's sparkling performance as because it had received international status. Five years later this growth was recognized by the boat's selection for the Olympics. Originally designed for construction in developed plywood, *Tornados* are now principally built in glassfibre, although moulded plywood is again becoming fashionable.

Length: 6100 mm
Beam: 3050 mm
Sailarea: 21·83 sq m
Weight: 145 kg (minimum)

It is perhaps more appropriate to say of catamarans than any other racing boat that the secret of good boatspeed lies in control of the boat at all times. This is because the relative speed of the boat is higher and the percentage increase in speed can make far bigger gaps between boats than in single-hulled boat-racing. Control of a *Tornado* depends entirely on how the boat is built and set up. Many of the races I have won have been won before I have even gone afloat, by having the boat set up so that nothing can go wrong, particularly at crucial moments during the race.

First, it is important that the hulls should be stiff. Since we built the prototype *Tornado* in my boatyard we have constantly looked for ways of making hulls stiffer. We started with developed ply hulls, torturing the ply into the hull sections after fixing the angle along the keel line. Then, as demand increased, we began to manufacture in glassfibre. I have spent many hours experimenting with various glassfibre lay-ups in order to get the stiffest possible hulls while keeping the weight down to the minimum and the ends light. As each new technological development became available commercially I examined the best way in which it could be used, if at all. Now I have reverted to moulded wooden hulls, which I believe I can build stiffer and lighter than by any of the reinforced plastics methods.

Around the main beam attachment point the hull must be very strong, as it must be around the after beam fixing too. The wringing strains here are very high, and it is also important that the two hulls should be prevented from

Beating to windward, CORK 1975.

flexing independently, because this affects the whole rig – and unless this is stable, a loss of power which destroys boatspeed will result. I have experimented with the beam attachments on the *Tornado* ever since our first crude efforts, which had two straps on each beam end bolted through to the gunwales of the hulls. I still think this is one of the most effective methods, but as a manufacturer I have been looking for ways of improving it cosmetically. The earliest ideas of through-bolting the beam itself were not successful because they allowed the beam to twist in its seating and thus the hulls worked independently. Now I have devised a keyway system which ensures that the beams are locked into their seating; the stress is now between the seating and the hull. By making the seating an integral part of the hull the problems are largely eliminated.

The rudders and centreboards are just as important as the hulls. With the high speeds of a *Tornado,* the drag of a badly-sectioned or badly-finished foil can make a difference of minutes in the time taken around an Olympic course. I take special care of these items, making sure, in the case of rudders, that they are kept in foam-lined bags, custom-made for the job, so that they are not dented or scratched; the hours spent making them perfect are easily wasted unless they are properly looked after. Centreboards, too, I always check, to see that the leading edges have not been damaged and that they are fully housed and protected inside the cases before coming ashore.

No matter how well you look after centreboards and rudders, there is always a chance that they will go 'off'. Warping is difficult to prevent and immediately alters their aerofoil sections, making them less efficient. If this occurs they must be scrapped. It is easy to determine when a centreboard or rudder is no longer any use: it will start to vibrate at high speed and set up a distinct humming sound. To find the offending foil, lift one at a time while sailing, and when the humming stops the culprit is found. Problems arise when two go wrong simultaneously!

With a stiff hull system, getting the rig right is not too difficult. Remember, however, that the forestay of a *Tornado* is only kept stiff by the tension in the mainsheet; the shroud angles do not allow the shrouds to exert much aft pull on the hounds, and this is one of the reasons why good speed to windward in a breeze is best obtained by feathering the boat slightly, rather than letting go the mainsheet every time the boat is hit by a gust. It is the stability of the rig that is important as there is a heavy penalty to pay in the form of drag over a flapping rig. It is bad enough when sails flap individually, far worse when the rig pants.

Control of the mainsail for various wind strengths can be obtained by using different battens, rotating the mast, and controlling the tension in the diamond stays. The stronger it blows the more the diamonds should be slacked when on the wind, in order to allow the rotated mast to bend and thereby flatten the sail. To encourage the fullness to return for the downwind legs the rotation of the mast should be lessened, so that the mast bends less in the fore and aft plane. For lighter weather the diamond stays should be set up harder.

Though jibs only provide a small part of the rig in terms of area, they are, nonetheless, most important since they provide the lead for the rig and their relationship to the mainsail determines the power available from the rig and therefore the boatspeed. Because they are so tall and narrow the jibs appear to twist considerably. What is important is that the luff should present the same angle to the wind all the way up, with perhaps just a little falling off – say 3 to 5 degrees maximum – to allow for wind shear. Since the *Tornado* spends much of its racing life with the wind apparently forward of the beam, the important thing about sheeting the jib is that it should be barber-hauled outboard and forwards for reaching.

Only by doing so can the relationship between jib and mainsail be kept in harmony.

Physical strength is important for sailing a *Tornado*. The loads on the sheets are heavier than those of a monohull with sails of the same size, because the higher speed of the boat increases the apparent wind. The number of parts in the mainsheet of a *Tornado* is therefore greater than in a monohull with a similarly-sized mainsail. Equally important is co-ordination between helmsman and crew. *Tornado* sailing is a knife-edge exercise and the difference between being in the groove and out of it is enormous. As soon as the lee bow starts to bury on a reach *both* sheets must be eased together, and the only way to get this kind of co-ordination is to sail as often as possible with a regular crew. I have sailed with my brother-in-law John Osborn for many years, and we react in virtually the same way to everything that goes on in the boat.

To get the best speed out of a *Tornado* the boat must be properly balanced. Too much heeling may look all right in an after-shave advertisement, but the instant the weather hull comes out of the water the boat loses efficiency. The ideal is for the weather hull just to kiss the surface. In light weather almost the converse is true, however, and you will have to

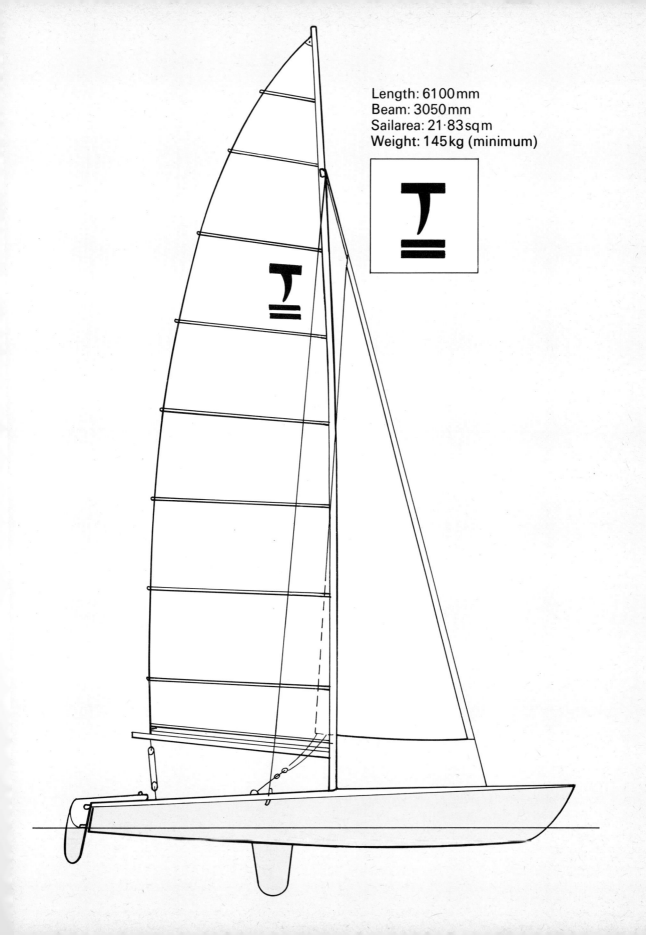

Length: 6100 mm
Beam: 3050 mm
Sailarea: 21·83 sq m
Weight: 145 kg (minimum)

encourage heeling somewhat to try to 'unstick' the weather hull; and then every little gust will mean that the crew has to move up from the lee hull.

Downwind sailing is difficult because you have to sail at the furthest offwind point without the rig stalling. It requires great concentration and ability to read the tell-tales on the mainsail; the crew must keep the jib in perfect

harmony with the mainsail. This point is scarcely practised at all by the catamaran sailor just out for a sail, but it is probably the most important of all on the race course. More places are won and lost downwind than upwind, and the ability to combine top boatspeed at the right angle with the reading of a tactical compass brings first place at the leeward mark.

A start at the 1975 pre-Olympic CORK regatta. The boat in the foreground will soon suffer from the dirty wind of the boat to windward. Perhaps the next best placed is G 452, which has clear air.

Enterprise

Mike McNamara

Chapter 11

Endeavour Trophy winner, 1965; National 12 Champion and Burton Trophy winner, 1969; Lark Champion, 1971; Albacore National Champion, 1973 and 1975; Enterprise National Championships, 3rd in 1968 and 1975; as crew, Enterprise National Champion 1967, Endeavour Trophy winner 1967, Enterprise World Champion 1971. Sailmaker.

The *Enterprise* was initially sponsored by the *News Chronicle* and has become one of the most successful of Jack Holt's designs. That almost twenty thousand have been built reflects its suitability for family racing, though this description hardly fits its performance at the top. Designed to be built at home, it has a double-chined hull very like a round-bilged boat. The class progressed from all-wood beginnings to today's glassfibre and composite examples, now as common as the all-wood versions, and alloy spars have become the norm rather than the exception.
Length: 4039mm
Beam: 1613mm (maximum)
Sailarea: 10·5sqm
Weight: 90·25kg (minimum)

The *Enterprise* is one of the strictest one-designs. Thus a fair shape achieved within the building tolerances will go as fast as any rival's. The scandal of the Section 2 and 4 measurements has subsided, and there now seems to be little exploitation of the building tolerances. Boats from the leading builders all go at the same speed. The rig is the most important aspect of boatspeed. Lack of control over the deck-stepped mast and the long boom means that sails are simple in concept; for that very reason such control as can be achieved has to be utilized to the full.

Because hull shapes are so similar, it is the details that are important. The finish on the hull must be given great attention; luckily the large flattish sections help both painting and polishing. It is essential to use the maximum amount of shaping and fairing allowed on the keel and bilge keels. It is also important to fair in the selfbailers, which must not be recessed or stick out proud from the hull. I prefer chines as sharp as possible, especially towards the transom. The junction between the bottom of the boat and the transom must be really sharp. Unless these two conditions are met, the flow of water from the hull will be seriously impaired.

Great care should be taken to get the centreboard slot gasket right. It must seal the bottom of the boat for two reasons: water going up into the centreboard box will cause drag on the boat, and, secondly, when reaching in a strong breeze or going to windward in a

On the Thames at Hammersmith.

lumpy sea-water will pour into the boat.

The profile of the centreboard and rudder is one-design and the section is limited to tapering only 2 inches from the edge. This means that only a primitive attempt may be made to aerofoil the blades. The leading edges should be rounded and faired back into the main body of the fin. The aft edges should be tapered to a razor-sharp edge. It is very difficult to maintain these razor edges, especially that of the centreboard, since this extends into the boat as the case is not topped. The best centreboards and rudders are made of solid or laminated strip mahogany; second-best are those made of 16-'strand' shatter-proof plywood. Whichever is used, it is essential that the boards be stiff. Incidentally, the rudder stalls easily after a roll or on a flat out plane – beware!

Stiffness is essential in both spars. Because the mast is deck-stepped with high hounds it is difficult to control. In the past, heavy and large sections were considered necessary. Recently, the class rules have been amended to allow spreaders; diamonds are also allowed, but these do not seem to work properly and have never found favour. Like most of the front-runners in the *Enterprise* fleet, I use spreaders and even those who have the older, stiffer sections should fit them. Mast sections may have become lighter or thinner but they should still be stiff. Spreaders are more important on *Enterprise* masts than on floor-stepped masts as there is no other resistance to the sideways thrust of the kicking strap when reaching. Experiments are still going on to determine the optimum height of the spreaders, but I like mine halfway between the hounds and the deck. They deflect the shrouds outwards $1\frac{1}{2}$ inches and forwards by a little over 1 inch. The sideways bend concerns me more than the fore and aft bend of the mast. If the mast is too rigid sideways, which is ideal for a tight leech and off-wind speed, the mast will not 'pant' while the boat is bouncing over the waves when going to windward, and a lot of speed is lost because the slot becomes congested.

Too much sideways stiffness in the mast is characterized by excessive backwinding of the mainsail and a boat that heels easily. It is therefore absolutely essential that the leeward shroud should go slack in quite light winds so that the mast can move to windward. The rigging must be tightened as the wind increases; since the class rules forbid the adjustment of shrouds while racing, the rigging is tightened by tensioning the jib halyard. Unless this is done there will be excessive jib luff sag, and the resulting sloppiness in the rig ruins performance. For that reason, too, the heel of the mast

Length: 4039 mm
Beam: 1613 mm (minimum)
Sailarea: 10·5 sqm
Weight: 90·25 kg (minimum)

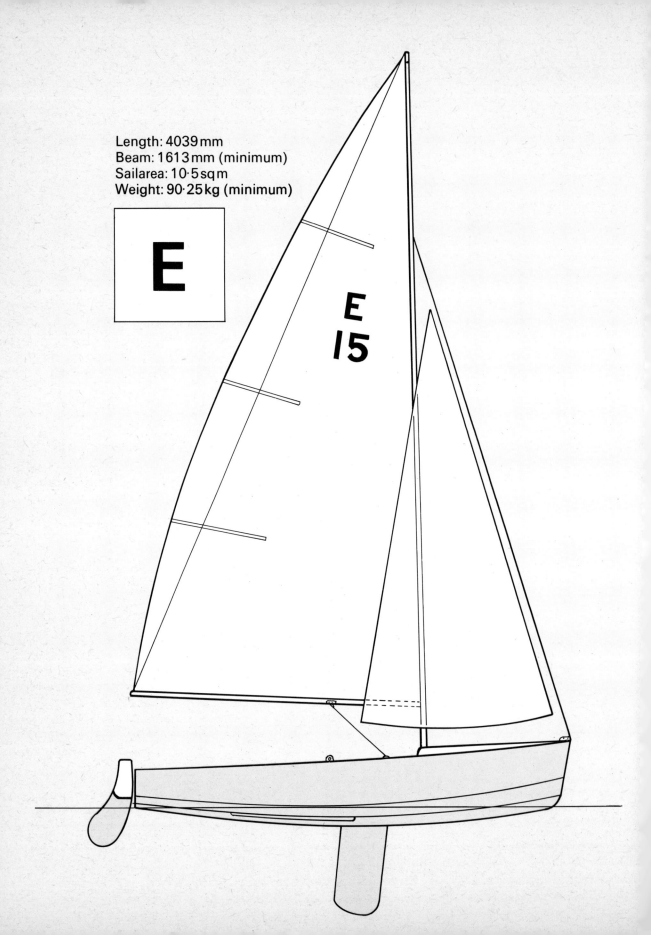

must fit tightly into the step. This is all too often neglected and with the heavy compression the hole in the wooden step soon becomes enlarged. Protecting it with metal or Tufnol will prevent this.

The boom must be very stiff. Large-sectioned ones are best, as the mainsail foot is relatively long and aft sheeting is all that is allowed by the class rules. Because the kicking strap is the main tool for controlling sail shape, the loads imposed on the boom have to be quickly transferred to the sail. It is difficult to get a section both stiff and light enough; if it is heavy, the boom will tend to drag the mainsail leech down, particularly in light weather.

Class rules require that the jib sheeting be confined to the side decks a minimum distance out from the centreline. Because of this, the modern full-cut, close-sheeting jibs which are allowed to twist off cannot be used on an *Enterprise*. As the jib sheeting angle is so wide, the sail must be reasonably flat – if it is too full the boat cannot point. The head of the jib is particularly significant; if it is too full the slot is closed, yet if it is too flat the whole top quarter of the sail flaps when the sheet is eased on a close reach in light weather.

Since there is no spinnaker, the jib cannot be merely a windward-going sail: it has to be efficient off the wind as well. Adjustable barber haulers are banned, and the reaching hooks that are allowed are rarely used. It is therefore absolutely essential that instantly adjustable fairleads with vertical jam cleats are fitted.

The large foot droop in the jib must be set by making the bottom full, otherwise the cloth outside the straight line will flap. It is easy to oversheet the bottom, but this is better than having the top too free. Tell-tales a quarter of the way down from the head help to obtain the right setting downwind; this should aim for efficiency in the middle, in the hope that the top and bottom will not hinder too much. To windward the foot droop curls up along the straight line, and no attempt can be made to set it unless the wind is very light. The jib is very critical of its setting; it is hard to get the leech eased when going to windward without causing the top to collapse and equally hard to stop the top flapping when off the wind. Constant vigilance on the crew's part is vital.

Even more critical is the shape of the mainsail. With problems in controlling the flexibility of the mast and boom, there is a limit to the amount of camber and the position of the flow. The mast bend will not be able to remove too much fullness and the sail will be too baggy for beating to windward. On the other hand, if the leech is too flat and does not hook

enough the sideways bend on the mast reduces the downwind speed.

The maximum point of flow is between a third and half of the way back into the sail. It is further back lower down and is proportionally flatter to cut down backwind. Above the jib the flow moves further forward, since more of the fullness consists of luff curve than of seam shaping; thus it can be removed by mast bend. The heeling forces are greater higher up in the sail so that fullness has to be removed from there first.

I use the kicking strap to control the fullness of the mainsail by the mast bend and adjust it all the time to tighten or slacken the leech. In this way the mainsheet track is rarely used. With a powerful kicker the mainsheet's duty is purely to control the angle of the boom to the centreline of the boat. I never pin the boom down with the mainsheet as this has to be tweaked all the time to keep the boat upright. It is imperative to coax and persuade the boat and to prevent it from heeling – once heeled, it is dead. As a gust hits, I use what I can, then ease the mainsheet to get rid of the excess and then sheet in again when I can. The traveller is never further out than a foot from the centreline; in this

There are many faults here: too much heel because the helmsman is not sitting out correctly; too much fullness in the mainsail which could be corrected by tensioning the cunningham; and an ineffective kicking strap.

position the majority of the leech chord is parallel to the centreline. As the wind decreases the leech must be eased, so the traveller is pulled in to the centre and the kicker and mainsheet eased.

Thus the kicking strap is the most important fitting in an *Enterprise*. It must be used brutally in a fresh breeze to flatten the sail.

If the toe-straps are badly positioned, the shape of the side decks and the position of the side seats can make sitting out agonising. The toe-straps should be fastened on to the centreplate case knee and then lead forward and aft to the two thwarts with adjustment beyond these. Tighter toe-straps are needed inland in gusty conditions.

The jib stick is very useful if properly used. On most boats, however, its eye is too high up the mast, and this forces the clew of the jib down and tightens the jib leech, which in turn stops the air from escaping. The eye should be placed 9 inches above the heel of the mast.

The *Enterprise's* keel shape and shoulders make it roll tack well. If you find that the first few feet after the tack are spent head to wind, this is because there is too much rake on the mast, which has moved the centre of effort aft and has allowed the boat to have its head while the helmsman fights to regain control of the rudder. Masts are, therefore, generally more upright than in other boats of similar size. If, with the sail set, the boom is horizontal or the end of the boom is less than 4 inches above the horizontal, then the rake is right.

Downwind in a breeze the *Enterprise* has some peculiar habits. It pretends to nose-dive after a gybe and the crew tend to move aft unnecessarily to correct this. On a run the 'death roll' can be cured by putting down some centreboard and sheeting the mainsail in a little more.

A good crew can contribute much to success in *Enterprise*-racing. The boat responds so well if it is upright, really upright, and that is very much the crew's province. Most people sit too far forward with the crew jammed tight against the shrouds. This trims the boat down by the bow and eases the stern out of the water. This may help in the very lightest of airs, but it does not work in a breeze: the full waterline length is not used and the boat slams into the waves, and both helmsman and crew are uncomfortable. I find that if the helmsman and crew move back 6 inches this is about right for most wind conditions. With more wind they should move further aft.

Enterprise owners can make few choices in the construction of their boats, and there is no doubt that the original plywood is best. A bow tank rather than a bag should be chosen for buoyancy. The bulkhead gives added strength where it is most needed and reduces the crushing loads of the shrouds.

OK

Dick Batt

Chapter 12

OK National Champion 1975, runner-up 1974; Endeavour Trophy runner-up 1975. Sailmaker.

The *OK* dinghy was developed in the late 1950s because Axel Damgaard wanted a cheap single-hander that would plane. Damgaard was a *Pirat* class sailor, and it is to this class that the *OK* owes her sail plan. Knud Olsen drew the hull lines, and it was immediately realized that the *OK* would make an ideal trainer for the larger *Finn* class. Despite this the *OK* progressed in its own right because it was easy to build. The boats are constructed of plywood, some glued with glass tape, of glassfibre and of composite materials, most by their owners. The unstayed cantilever rig with its heavily roached sail has to be 'universal' for success and spars are now almost all aluminium alloy. The class was granted full international status in 1974.

Length: 4000 mm
Beam: 1420 mm
Sailarea: 8·36 sq m
Weight: 72 kg (minimum)

Rig, hull, centreboard and rudder, in that order, are the most important factors in the *OK* for producing boatspeed. The rig is by far and away the most important; it is probably the mast rather than the sail that is the controlling point. The rig must be the minimum weight and must be flexible enough to give proper control of the leech tension and the sail draft. A versatile rig is an absolute must. None of the top competitors in the world has two sails for competition use, except identical spares; only a few use two masts. The hull is less important. The minimum weight must be adhered to, the bottom must be stiff and the finish light. Both the centreboard and rudder must be smooth, stiff, reliable and, once again, light. The *OK* is light, blunt and unstable. Problems arise in finding ways of getting power from the rig in light and sloppy conditions, and the rig must also be sufficiently versatile to provide a 'staggerless' ride in high winds and waves.

Several important factors govern the speed of the hull itself. Since there is no all-up sailing weight, every item must be as light as possible, including the mast and boom, the centreboard and rudder and all those little extra items such as ropes and control lines. Lack of weight in the *OK* is one of the factors leading to success. But in getting the boat as light as possible some things must not be sacrificed. The boat must be stiff, both torsionally and in the skin; and it must also be fair.

The *OK* hull is constructed very much like a box with compartments; because of this and because there are no compression strains from shrouds

Running in very light winds on the Thames at Hammersmith.

and forestay the topsides can be light. The box construction is sufficient to resist the torsion from the cantilevered mast. This allows slightly thicker ply to be used to stiffen the bottom of the hull. Most boats are built flat and straight, straight in the run with straight bow waterlines; there are wide tolerances, however, and their careful use does seem to make a difference. Some boats have recently been constructed too round, especially in the bow. This produces a tendency to pitch, though they are very fast downwind. I favour a conservative boat shape with a slight arc in the bottom and only a slight increase in the rounding of the bow. This shape will be a good all-round performer.

A good finish is of paramount importance. The whole hull cannot be too smooth, and it is an easy enough shape to rub down. The keel band should be faired in and there are no slot rubbers to worry about. Because of this it is important to have a centreboard which fits tightly into the centreplate case; this helps to stop turbulence in the case.

Getting a good rudder is easy. I use anti-shatter plywood as thick as the class rules allow and make up my rudder as a fixed blade with the fittings bolted as far apart as possible. The further apart they are the less is the strain imposed on them. The design shape is not good, but there is no way round it. In addition, the chord ratio is too thin and prevents you getting a good aerofoil shape on the rudder. I merely round the front edge to avoid stalling and then fair the trailing edge to a sharp point from about halfway back along the chord. This provides me with a good thickish blade which has very little flexibility, despite the rake.

The only way I know of making the centreboard sufficiently stiff is to use laminated mahogany strips. In order to get a good trailing edge I pour epoxy resin into a deep groove in the centre of the back of the board, before I begin to shape it. Thus, as I plane down the board to an aerofoil shape, the resin provides an additional guide. It also provides a strong back edge to the centreboard. The trouble with the *OK* centreboard is that it is a blunt, stubby, horrible shape, and aerofoiling is only part of the solution. Far more important is that it should be stiff in the handle and that the handle should fit the case exactly. I use a hard aluminium strip to stiffen the centreboard handle, and I stiffen heavily that part of the inside centreboard case on which the handle bears. This stops the centreboard from wobbling at the tip. I take a great deal of care to get a perfect finish on both the centreboard and rudder; in this, there is no substitute for hard work. Two-can polyurethane white paint, about eight

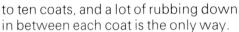
to ten coats, and a lot of rubbing down in between each coat is the only way.

For best boatspeed the weight and centre of gravity of the mast must be right on the minimum limits. Almost without exception aluminium alloy has taken over where once wood ruled, for it is vital that the mast material should have a high recovery rate in flexing. In addition, aluminium has a constancy of recovery that a wooden mast cannot match, especially in varying heat and humidity. The boom, once again of aluminium, must be as stiff and as light as possible; with low head clearance a boom with a rounded bottom has a slight advantage over one with sharp corners.

Boats are now going faster with masts that are stiffer than before, stiffer, that is, between the black bands. The greatest flexibility in the mast is now around the boom area and below the deck. This allows sails to be cut flatter since they have to accommodate less deflection in the length of the mast. In addition, most of the leech tension is gained by bending the strong 'root' of the mast, using the whole length of the mast as a lever. This gives good recovery to the rig when gust and lull quickly succeed one another, as well as better control of the leech tension with the mainsheet. In order to achieve good windward performance it is essential that the lower part of the mast is stiff laterally. The tip, however, should deflect sideways progressively as the wind increases so that the leech of the sail is opened evenly as required. Masts of this type also stand more upright downwind and thereby lose less power from flexing in their length – the relative hinging low down stops when the mainsheet is eased.

Most rigs will cope with a breeze; the problems come on days when there is not enough wind for the size of the sea. It is difficult to get the necessary extra power to push a light blunt box over lumpy water, out of a rig that is also capable of handling a Force 6 breeze with only 170 lb sitting out over the side. It is vital to use the cunningham, even more so to understand exactly what it does. The luff tension of the sail controls the angle of the big roached leech: more luff tension and the leech is open; ease the luff tension and the leech hooks back. The rest of the sail control is entirely in the mainsheet and must be carefully used. It is not worth wasting energy playing see-saws on every passing wave and fiddling with a collection of unnecessary controls.

The sail is cut on the flat side; it is vital for the flow to be cut in the seams of the sail so that when the mainsheet is eased in lighter winds the fullness does not move forward towards the mast. In cutting my own

Length: 4000 mm
Beam: 1420 mm
Sail area: 8·36 sq m
Weight: 72 kg (minimum)

K1792

sails I exploit the measurements as much as I can to get a big roach; this helps to make the rig versatile.

My own boatspeed improved as I got rid of control systems. I once sailed with a profusion of them, now I have only a mainsheet, cunningham and traveller control on my boat. The

kicking strap is a fixed wire. Over the years I have managed to get rid of sail outhaul, sail inhaul, adjustable downhaul, plate controls, adjustable kicking strap and even the compasses (because the boat is not really steady enough to use them). Certainly, without the extra controls there is more time to think about using the boat and its rig effectively. The controls that I do have are all bolted on and they work at all times. The mainsheet is 8 mm in diameter; it has a 3 : 1 purchase over small roller blocks and is made bearable by the use of a ratchet block on the traveller. The mainsheet then runs freely offwind; when going to windward it is always cleated, except in light and variable winds.

The rules governing the *OK's* side decks are fairly open and must be exploited to the full. Comfort is of major importance in a small single-hander, and with correctly-shaped side decks and properly-adjusted toe-straps the *OK* can be made reasonably comfortable. If you are not comfortable you will not be able to concentrate and other boats will go faster.

The *OK* sails best with the centreboard a long way down. It has to

John Dawson-Edwards in complete balance to windward; note the bend low down in the mast.

be raised in light to medium winds on the reaches and runs, and perhaps a little when beating in very strong winds. For the rest of the time it should be kept well down, as it helps to dampen the roll on the run.

The position of the helmsman in the fore and aft plane is also important. The crew weight of an *OK* equals its hull weight and so moving forward or aft a few inches achieves far more than worrying about weight distribution in the hull during construction.

I endeavour to keep my weight on the centre of pitching, which is around the back edge of the centreboard case, so as to waste as little energy as possible. In addition, I lift and drop my weight as the boat pitches. In light airs it does not pay to move forward, unlike many other dinghies. It is far better to sit comfortably and concentrate. The *OK* likes to plane level, so that only bow-burying or broaching should force the skipper towards the stern. On the run sit as far forward as is conducive to safety.

OKs have been quick to adopt one useful item of gear from the *Finns* – the J.C. strap. This is a shockcord running through the bow fairlead and coming back on each side of the mast to a point about half-way along the boom. Its purpose is purely to hold the boom out offwind, since the *OK* has no crew to do this.

103

Fireball

Dick Jobbins

Chapter 13

Fireball National Champion, 1974;
Contender World and National
Champion, 1970. Boatbuilder.

The scow form, popular enough on
North American lakes and in
Australasian *Moths,* only caught on
elsewhere when Peter Milne designed
the *Fireball* in 1962. Primarily intended
for home construction, most of the ten
thousand plus boats now in existence
all over the world have been built by
their owners. The double-chined hull
was designed to be sailed with 3 to 5
degrees of heel and is very responsive
to being in the right groove. The trapeze
and the spinnaker were later additions
to the *Fireball.* The freedom of the jib
measurement in this class brought
much early experimentation; the
sheeting angle of the jib is probably
narrower than in any other dinghy class
– and with great effect.

Length: 4928 mm
Beam: 1359 mm
Sailarea: 11·43 sq m (main and jib),
13·01 sq m (spinnaker)
Weight: 79·4 kg (minimum)

Preparation and maintenance are
the secrets of success as far as
boatspeed in a *Fireball* is concerned.
Get it right and keep it right and there
will be few problems afloat. The fewer
the problems, the harder the boat can
be driven; the greater the concentration,

The fleet shortly after the start in the European
Championship at Hayling Island, 1975.

the better the results. It all boils down to
a simple philosophy, but one which has
stood me in good stead in the past.

Running a boatbuilding firm that
produces *Fireballs* keeps me on my toes
as far as development in the class is
concerned, and, despite all the shouting
about the *Fireball* being a one-design
class, I think it has to be considered as a
development class. The framework of
the class rules is such that there is a
great deal of freedom in the way that
the boats are constructed, the way they
are fitted out, the way they are rigged
and the way that the sails are cut.
Occasionally there is a major
breakthrough somewhere and then the
whole class tends to follow the fashion.
The real thinker will evaluate a new
development and try to find a way of
improving it.

Without a good hull you start with
a handicap. My own opinion about
glassfibre hulls is well known: they last
longer in prime condition. Today's
glassfibre hulls have resulted from
progressive development, and despite
the fact that the *Fireball,* with its flat
sections, was designed originally to be
built in plywood, the glassfibre boats
are every bit as competitive as their
most sophisticated wooden
counterparts. The hull must be stiff;
even in the flat areas this can be ensured
by careful use of microballoons in the
lay-up and by using woven glass

rovings instead of chopped strand mat. Care must be taken to reduce the amount of cloth towards the ends of the hull; with this the amount of resin is also reduced. The longitudinal stiffness of the hull is ensured by continuing a spine forward and aft from the centreboard case to the bow and stern transoms.

The decks too help to provide stiffness in the hull, yet they must be kept as light as possible. Stiffeners and deckbeams can be eliminated altogether by the use of high-density foam laid up between the glass laminates. Once again the foam is tapered off towards the bow and stern. The mast gate is closed at the aft end of the partners and the back of the foredeck runs out to the chainplates. A part-bulkhead carries down the side of the boat to the chainplate, across the chine panel and on to the bottom connecting up with the plate case. Verticals from the mast partners to the plate case keep this area rigid even in the heaviest breezes, when the strains on the shrouds and the compression of the mast are greatest.

With a glassfibre hull a perfect finish is within everyone's capabilities. On a new boat it is simply a matter of wax polishing. On an older boat that has been scratched, the blemishes must be filled with gel coat and the offending area rubbed down and burnished to match the rest before the wax polishing is begun.

One of the principal factors affecting the boatspeed of a *Fireball* is the centreboard slot gasket. This must be properly fitted, or the swirling water in the case will use up much of the kinetic energy from the rig otherwise available for driving the boat forwards. The best gaskets are made from plastic sheeting cut so that there is 5 inches in front of the platecase opening and 4 inches aft. The sheet is then stuck to the hull and slit from end to end of the slot with a razor blade against a straight edge. The slot should be extended 1 inch forward and 1 inch aft to a $\frac{3}{16}$ inch diameter hole drilled in the plastic sheet. To give added protection I double the first 14 inches of this plastic gasket, putting a 'V' in the slot at the aft end. Carefully looked after, this type of gasket should last a whole season.

The 'rails' on the bottom and chine of the *Fireball* must also be cared for. The protective brass strips on these can easily get bent, and this will affect the speed of the boat. This usually happens when the boat is ashore, and so I have a rule that the boat must touch nothing but the water or a well-padded and fitted trailer chock.

Too many people race badly prepared boats that let them down during races, and so I always emphasize that maintenance is all-important in

Length: 4928 mm
Beam: 1359 mm
Sailarea: 11·43 sq m (main and jib),
13·01 sq m (spinnaker)
Weight: 79·4 kg (minimum)

winning races. Every fitting, every screw, nut and bolt, every rope and wire, must be checked before every race. Gear failure is inevitable if nothing is serviced.

Spars should be fairly stiff. The heavier you are the stiffer they should be, though it is true to say that in a *Fireball* terribly limber spars do not work well. To tune the rig for different winds it is necessary to impose a certain amount of pre-bend in the mast with the mast ram and the kicking strap. My latest innovation is a 'muscle box' on the foredeck in front of the mast which is capable of pushing and pulling, thus giving greater control of the mast bend. This can readily be adjusted underway and the whole rig kept in tune with the wind conditions. Since I prefer not to use a mainsheet traveller (I have the mainsheet blocks on the top of the centreboard case in the centre of the boat instead), it is essential to use a very powerful kicking strap. A 4:1 purchase on a 6:1 lever is ideal for the *Fireball.*

The mast must be kept as clean as possible; for this reason all the hound fittings should be inside the spar. The shrouds will go through a $\frac{3}{16}$-inch hole and the trapeze wires through a $\frac{1}{8}$-inch one. I dispense with a jib halyard altogether and instead have a short wire strop fitted in the same way as the shrouds; to give adjustment a pin-hole plate is spliced to the end. The absence

of the jib halyard also ensures free running of the spinnaker halyard.

After every race I check all the shrouds and halyards, particularly at their terminals, and reject and replace anything that is the slightest bit suspect.

Booms must be relatively stiff to take the mainsheet and kicker loads. A big-section, thin-walled tube is best with the outboard end cut away underneath. This allows the top to flex upwards in very strong winds and automatically free the leech of the mainsail.

The spinnaker pole vang system and the pole ends themselves must work without a hitch every time. With the long pole of the *Fireball,* a system with the spinnaker boom permanently rigged is best. The pole flies away alongside the main boom when not in use. An all-wire vang with a keyhole ring over the boom is both simple and efficient. The height of the sheave box on the mast is important; when the spinnaker is not in use the keyhole ring should be at the same height as the main boom – the downhaul part of the vang being connected to the shockcord inside the mast. With this set-up the pole cannot be lost and there is, therefore, no need to carry a spare in the boat.

There have been more fancy cuts of sails in the *Fireball* class than in any

other. Many of the people who sail them are fashion-followers, and I believe the sailmakers have traded on them. I prefer a conservatively-cut sail, although lately I have tended to go for sails with the fullness further aft. In light weather the ideal is to have the maximum fullness of the mainsail just forward of the inboard ends of the battens and the jib fullness at the mid-chord. Both sails should be tight-leeched. The same sails can be used for heavy weather by tuning the sails with the mast. By pulling out the mainsail to the maximum on the boom and careful use of the cunningham, the sail can be flattened with additional mast bend and the leech will also be freed. The jib leech is freed by moving the fairlead slightly aft and allowing the jib to twist off at the head. In anything of a seaway fullish sails are important to give the *Fireball* sufficient drive. In flat waters, flatter sails can be used to advantage. It is important to have a good working relationship with one's sailmaker; deal with someone in the class whom you can see regularly to discuss your problems. Sails can almost invariably be improved.

Because of the reaching performance of the *Fireball*, it is

Here Dick Jobbins and Paul van Looke are spinnaker reaching, the forté of this pair. Note the balls of the crew's feet on the gunwale, ready to move fore and aft with the waves; and once again the neutral helm showing a boat in balance.

important to have a spinnaker cut for that point of sailing. The class rules allow only one spinnaker to be carried, and for that reason, too, it should be made as light as possible, preferably in $\frac{3}{4}$ ounce material. It will not last forever, however, because the constant pulling on the retrieving line will begin to stretch the sail at the point at which the retrieving line is attached, and distort it. It will last a long time in top racing conditions if it is not hauled up to dry with one leech held tight and the whole thing allowed to flap. That only has sailmakers rubbing their hands in joy!

Because of its shape the *Fireball* does need some special handling. It cannot be driven hard into waves like some boats with fine entries; instead it has to be nursed over the waves. By moving his weight fore and aft the crew will help this. He can lift the bow over the wave by moving aft and force the boat to go down the back of it by moving forward. Reaching in a seaway, 'gunwale running' by the crew can almost double the boat's speed down a leg. A week or so spent board-surfing will help almost any dinghy sailor to improve his downwind techniques in a seaway. Nor is it only the big waves that help; the small ones on light-weather days make a dramatic difference, too.

Running should be avoided except in strong winds. The *Fireball* goes much faster if it is pointed up 10 degrees or so and tacked downwind to take advantage of the shifts. The extra speed gained more than makes up for the extra distance travelled.

Chapter 14
Elemental tactics

A race must be planned, and planning depends on the conditions of the day. Everything is variable: the wind, the waves, the amount the wind is shifting, the angle of the start line to the wind, and the course that is to be steered. The discussions in this book are based on a triangular Olympic course, with a 90-degree turn at the gybe mark, a windward/leeward round, followed by a beat to the finish. Sailors have different theories about how the problems should be tackled, and of course the classes themselves vary, their boats having different sailing characteristics. Some classes are more tactically aware than others; generally, the faster the boat the more good elemental tactics are emphasized, the less hand-to-hand fighting. The questions posed cover basic techniques; though the champions sometimes repeat one another, there is value in their repetition.

How do you plan the windward leg? Does the strength of the wind make any difference?

Pattisson: Assuming I do not have to watch other competitors or close rivals, I tend to go up the centre, always making sure that my wind is clear. If it is blowing very hard and survival conditions prevail, tacking can lose you a lot of distance. In those conditions I tend to go one way or the other, concentrating on boatspeed and tacking only if it is really necessary.

Peter White: I ascertain the tide at the committee boat and at the outer distance mark (the pin) and then go up the first leg from the start before the race to familiarize myself with the conditions; in particular I try to evaluate

the windshifts or bends, studying the clouds as I do so. My tactics remain the same whatever the wind, except that in big seas it is essential to look for a flat patch in which to tack. I tack less in heavy weather because of the amount of time lost on each occasion the boat is put about.

Warren: First I consider the prevailing wind and how it is likely to shift, then the tide and how it will be running all over the leg. With this information I can choose the optimum course to the first mark, just as long as I can get clear wind.

McNamara: Since boatspeeds are similar, great use must be made of windshifts and of going the right way. I like to sail much of the first leg looking out for other boats going well. For that reason it is important to be able to sail the boat without having to think about speed; that part of sailing must be automatic. The stronger the winds, the harder the boat is to sail; the *Enterprise* is over-canvassed and so speeds vary more. The harder it is driven the faster it will go, so I try to tack less and concentrate more on the waves.

Batt: Often there is a bias to the beat, because of the wind or the tide. The various conflicting factors must be carefully assessed. If I think one side is preferable, I aim to get clear soon after the start so that I can tack towards that side at will. I try never to be too busy to assess the progress of other boats or too proud to act if I am obviously on the wrong side of the course. With practice you can sail automatically while having a good look at the rest of the fleet. The stronger the wind, the less I take notice and act on minor windshifts. Broader moves pay in bigger winds, and the relative effect of tide is less.

Jobbins: I sail at least half-way

up the first beat before the start so that I can evaluate the shifts and bends in the wind. Wind strength does make a difference, and in the stronger breezes I endeavour to herd the fleet the way I want them to go; in such conditions there is only one way to go, and if I can keep them all together I am confident of beating them through superior boatspeed. In light airs I pick my way clear of the bunches of boats. Clear wind is all important, together with luck.

Maynard: Before the start as much information as possible must be gathered about the conditions that will affect the race. What are the tidal effects, direction and strength, all over the course, and will they alter during the race? Will the land cause any permanent windbends? What about the wind itself, will it strengthen or fall? The windshift pattern is also important: is it steady, short swings or long ones, gradually veering or backing; if it is gusty, is it backing or veering in the gusts? All these facets have to be explored. The weather forecast should give some indication of the general pattern, the effect of a sea breeze for instance. A skipper must be able to categorize the information he receives; what is happening now, what is certain to happen, what is likely to happen, what could possibly happen, and finally, what is unlikely to happen. Then he will be able to plan his windward legs properly.

In an oscillating wind it is vital to get on the lifted tack as soon as possible after the start and to be among the first to pick up the next shift. This could mean making a start at the 'wrong' end of the line. Although this type of planning will help to increase a helmsman's chances of going the right

way up the beat, he must also be on the lookout for unforeseen changes in the conditions.

Wind strength has a definite effect on planning the windward legs. In light winds with little tide, it is most important to go for the areas of strongest wind. In large fleets, the wind is often lightest in the middle of the course; in this case sail to either wing and leave the middle-of-the-course tacker wallowing. In strong winds and choppy seas, a lot of ground can be lost in tacking, and, other things being equal, you should sail to the side of the course with the flattest water. In medium winds the fight for clear air is vital.

Eyre: Consult the tide chart to decide whether any significant gains can be made by biasing your course to one side or the other on the beat. Careful scrutiny of the weather forecast makes it possible to predict fairly accurately what the wind will do. I then plan to tack on the heading tack until I can just lay below the windward mark on the tack on which I expect a freer. Wind strength is only relevant if there are smooth stretches of water which allow the boat to be sailed faster.

Oakeley: Before any race it is important to check and note the bearing of the wind at five-minute intervals for all parts of the course, so that the pattern of the shifts becomes clear. Only rarely are the oscillations irregular. I often plan to start at the unfavoured end of a start line, knowing that soon, when the wind swings back and after tacking, I will become the windward boat of the fleet. Getting the oscillations right is the key to success to windward. The other important factor is how you tackle the seas, particularly when the wind is dropping. Use the stronger wind to go on the tack that takes you closest into the seas, so that when the wind drops further you will then be on the tack along the waves, which uses less of the boat's kinetic energy. If the wind is gusting the same principle applies: use the gusts to go into the waves and the lulls to go along them.

Reg White: Oscillations and general trends determine the way up the windward legs. For a *Tornado*, the strength of the wind does alter conditions a little. With fresh breezes you can concentrate on boatspeed rather than on shifts, whereas in light weather the shifts become paramount.

Crebbin: In international meetings there is very rarely any permanent reason for favouring one side of the course; the venues are chosen to eliminate this. A pattern of the temporary reasons for favouring one particular side of the course must therefore be established. In a top fleet it is important to sail the first beat as fast as possible without worrying about the other boats; it is rare to see a series winner going right out to one side in every race – tenth around the first mark every day is better than first one day and thirtieth the next. Wind strength is of little importance in planning a beat. Boatspeed is more easily lost by looking around, and in a *470* the reasons for tacking must be good, for a lot of ground is lost with every tack.

Bruce: On the first windward leg you should favour the right-hand side of the course, but without committing yourself completely; or you should favour the left, with the same reservation; or you should concentrate on the shifts. After evaluating what happened on the first, you can sail the second and subsequent beats with a total commitment to one side or the other; if you still can't commit yourself, you're back to playing the individual shifts again.

How do you plan to round the weather mark, assuming marks to port? Do varying wind strengths or the size of the fleet make any difference?

Crebbin: The decision can be left until fairly late, since it depends on where you are in the fleet. Near the front, there is generally more room and so the approach can be made on port, tacking at the last minute. If you are in the string of starboard tackers, you can only go as fast as the slowest, so it pays to arrive in the line as late as possible. Wind strength does matter, since it is easier to tack into a two-boat-length gap in Force 1 than in Force 5.

Bruce: The *Laser* tacks so quickly that it is mad to get involved with the starboard tack queue.

Reg White: In stronger winds the only way in is on starboard, but in light winds it is worth coming in on port and tacking almost at the mark. The number of boats in the fleet makes little difference, so long as you are up with the front-runners. Further back in the fleet it is hard to get into the line of starboard tackers; the further back you are, however, the more likely they will have overstood and you will be able to tack to leeward of them.

Pattison: I favour as short a starboard tack as possible in all wind strengths, thus avoiding the dirty wind for as long as possible. The bigger the fleet the more important this is.

Oakeley: Rounding the weather mark is only easy if you are in the lead. Down the fleet you are governed by what the other boats do. The long starboard tack to the mark is rarely successful; instead, a port tack laying 150 yards to leeward of the buoy is best. This also ensures that in a windshift you will not overstand the buoy; a very important point with a *Soling*.

Jobbins: So much depends on who you are covering and how many boats are close enough to give you trouble. Starboard it must be, but not for long.

Eyre: I approach the same way in all weathers; on starboard to windward of the others if the tide is adverse and to leeward if there is wind against tide. If the buoy is very close, positioning in relation to other boats is more important than clear wind.

Maynard: In the absence of any special tidal or wind factors, it is best to judge the main approach to the mark by deliberately understanding it so that you are fairly near the mark before making the final starboard tack approach. If you are in the middle of a big fleet a port tack lay-line approach is bad because of interference from the boats already on the reach and also on starboard tack. In strong winds over-stand slightly on the final approach so that a smooth and controlled rounding can be made. Overstand, too, in fickle winds, since a last-minute header can bring big problems to an over-accurate approach.

Peter White: The size of the fleet is irrelevant to tactics; your place in it is all that is important. If you are near the front an early starboard approach is good; the further back you are, the more important it is to stay on port until the last possible moment. In strong winds starboard tack with a slight amount of overstanding is a must.

McNamara: In a boat that tacks well you should concentrate on the windshifts and sneak in at the mark. If the fleet is big and the waves are large I would line up on starboard, over-standing slightly, so that I could crash through all the rough water at the mark. In a light boat there is no hope if you have to squeeze for the mark, as without the power on, the hull is easily knocked about.

Warren: Ideally, you should come in on starboard so that rounding is a simple manoeuvre, but in big fleets, if you are not leading, it is better to approach just to leeward on port. In heavier breezes it is best to overstand on starboard rather than tack from port at the mark.

Batt: The bigger the fleet, the more I tend to the long lay-line to the mark in order to avoid the cone of interference to leeward.

Does it make any difference if the mark is to be taken to starboard?

Warren: I always reckon to come in on port regardless of the size of the fleet.

Eyre: I always approach on starboard being careful not to overstand with a windward going current. In adverse tide I always aim to leave plenty of room to tack uptide of the mark.

Pattisson: Fortunately, this is not often seen in Olympic classes. I prefer to come in on a short port tack, and if I know I am nearly level with those coming in on starboard I will overstand a little so that I can bear away under them and still make the mark or they will tack before facing an issue with me.

Maynard: If you are sure that other boats will be near you at the weather mark, the best approach is a short starboard tack right on the lay-line, even overstanding it by a yard.

The helmsman of 19067 has just felt the effect of the dirty wind of the boat ahead. It has headed him and he is bearing away to keep his sail full. The wind will shortly revert to its original direction and then he must luff up to use it properly.

Even if there is a queue of similarly-minded starboard tackers right behind you, you will be able to luff hard at the mark and complete the tack without fouling anyone. In large fleets the approach to a mark to be rounded to starboard must be correct, even more than one to port. A whole string of starboard tackers can stop you from tacking on to the first reach, losing you a lot of hard-earned places. If you are forced in from the port lay-line, it is as well to overstand by several lengths, so as to avoid the chaos at the mark.

Jobbins: If you are in a large bunch the approach must be on starboard.

Batt: I prefer to overstand on port if I have to, rather than coming in on starboard and risking trouble from the boats behind. If I must come in on starboard I overstand just enough to shave the weather mark in a prolonged luff and tack.

Bruce: In a large fleet I go 30 to 50 yards to leeward of the mark on starboard and then overstand by a couple of lengths on port. In small fleets I come into the mark on starboard two or three boats to leeward of the mark.

McNamara: It is best to appoach on starboard, putting in a short hitch in advance so as to be able to do so. At the mark I luff violently to put the boat to windward out of harm's way and then tack smoothly on to port. Otherwise you have to overstand and come in on the port tack, ready to bear away under any starboard tackers, telling them loudly that they should not tack in your water. This tactic doesn't bear thinking about if the fleet is large, while it doesn't matter how big the fleet is if you approach on starboard.

Reg White: In a catamaran the approach must be from the port side, slightly overstanding to avoid getting caught in the starboard tack stack-up.

Oakeley: Rounding the weather mark to starboard is strictly for the birds. No race officer should be allowed to set such a course. The racing rules as they now stand do not allow this manoeuvre to be executed fairly.

Peter White: I opt for the starboard lay-line only if I am near the front; otherwise I overstand on port.

Crebbin: You can often get away with overstanding by one length on port and letting the boats on starboard tack inside you; but remember that they do not have to tack.

What is the ideal track from the weather mark to the gybe mark? Does it alter with wind strength?

Maynard: Ideally, it should be a straight line, but only for a clear leader. You should overstand the gybe mark by about a boat's length and bear away smoothly so that the gybe takes place just before the sail hits the buoy. The stronger the wind, the further you should be from the mark, purely for safety reasons. If other boats are present the ideal has to be scrapped. Rounding just ahead of an aggressive bunch of boats, you must luff to keep clear wind but then bear away again as soon as possible. If there is a big gap behind you and you are the last of the bunch at the weather mark, it might be worth bearing off sharply and sailing below the rhumb line to get into clear air. This will bring the advantage of being inside the bunch at the gybe, coming into the mark fast on a close reach. In light winds, however, do not try to break through to leeward: the windward boats will sail away on the puffs, which will be dissipated before they reach the leeward boats. In very strong winds it pays to work to leeward on the waves, leaving something in hand to luff up and survive the worst squalls.

Jobbins: The wave pattern makes a big difference. A planing boat on a reach can be used like a surf-board, and this makes such a great difference to speed that it outweighs other tactical advantages.

Warren: A straight line between the two buoys; if there were no other boats to consider, I would bear away slighly to allow an easier spinnaker hoist and come up above the line slightly before the gybe mark to allow an easier gybe. In light weather it pays to go high in the lulls and come down in the puffs. At the rear end of the fleet one has to go to leeward immediately and stay well to leeward of the rhumb line, coming up fast on the wing mark very late.

Eyre: The secret in any weather is to maintain clear wind at all times. Never attempt leeward overtaking at close quarters as you will lose ground relative to the rest of the fleet, even if you can pass fairly easily through the other boat's wind shadow.

Pattisson: The stronger the wind, the more I tend to luff above the rhumb line, which is the shortest course, if other boats make it necessary. Try, however, to get to leeward of the rhumb line two-thirds of the way down the leg in order to ensure that any overlap situation will benefit you.

Batt: The more boatspeed is related to waves, the more it pays to go to leeward. In sub-planing or flat-water planing, wind is all important and must be defended. Though tactics do not alter much whatever the wind strength, they do with waves. The more the boat can be forced or driven by the waves, the less important clear wind becomes.

Bruce: If you are leading but are being followed closely, sail high for 30 to 40 yards and establish a 'weather posture' in an attempt to discourage the second boat from attacking to weather. Likewise, if you are in second position and the leader has sailed directly for the mark, go high immediately after rounding. The lead boat is less likely to respond to a boat overtaking well to weather than to one nearby. In a *Laser* it is seldom worth sailing off to leeward, and never if the apparent wind is forward of abeam, or in a freshening or gusty wind. It can be worthwhile if the reach is very broad, as the 'pack' always sails very high in these conditions, scrapping for clear air.

McNamara: I would luff considerably to protect my weather if I know that this type of aggression will sort the other chap out. It doesn't pay to go to leeward – there are too many windshadows and wash. In really heavy weather take the leeward route, because the majority of the fleet will be doing 'the great circle' to the mark.

Reg White: It's all a matter of whether or not you can lay the mark without gybing in a catamaran. The stronger the wind the easier this is.

Oakeley: The straight line is right, but other competitors never let you go the right way. Clear wind is essential in all non-planing conditions.

Peter White: There are no definite rules. The major consideration is to keep clear of other boats.

Crebbin: If you are stuck with a large bunch, it is worth going to leeward, as that is the right side to be on at the gybe mark. This decision must be taken immediately; the longer it is put off the less successful it is likely to be. Ideally, a straight line is best, but factors such as tide, land promontories and wind shadows can alter this; the one thing that must be avoided at all costs is running dead to the mark. If you come in on a close reach you will have the best chance of an inside overlap. If you are outside a bunch, slow up, go across their sterns and be second round the mark, on the inside. In stronger winds free off in the slams and luff above the direct line in the lulls. The second part of the manoeuvre is perhaps the most important because you can be caught struggling to leeward of the rhumb line unable to make the mark with the spinnaker up at the finish of the leg.

What is the ideal track from the gybe mark to the leeward mark? Does it alter with the wind strength?

Eyre: At the gybe I always luff to windward of the next mark in order to secure an inside berth at the leeward buoy and to protect my wind from the boats behind. Approach the lee mark

wide and turn close to it to get the best advantage for the next windward leg: if you are pressed, don't worry; when taken close the inside berth will still leave you with a safe leeward position on the boat behind.

Warren: Hit the straight line again but get down close to the mark so that a swing up close to the mark keeps out the opposition.

Jobbins: Forget the opposition until you are near the mark – boatspeed

Starting, the seventh race of the Laser World Championship, Bermuda. Note, firstly, sag in the line – contrary to everyone's belief that there is a mid-field bulge; and secondly, the low density of starters at the 30 per cent positions. This is the precise moment of gunfire. The pin end mark has been reconstructed from other photo material. The boat astern and to leeward of Ian Bruce swore at him for at least 30 seconds, to get out of his way because he believed that Ian was over the line. Bruce's back transit was to the corner of a pink house with a verandah! Bruce believed that the left-hand side of the course was favoured but did not go all the way. Those that did, beat him to the weather mark although he still arrived fifth, high enough up to win the race. Photo – Hans Loffel.

is all important on the reaches – and go for the inside berth for the next windward leg.

McNamara: I always like to be well outside the leeward mark so that by rounding it gradually, and just missing it, I can use the extra speed gained on a reach to do a luff to windward to gain distance. If you try to round too vigorously, the boat stops.

Bruce: In light air it is important to get the position that enables you to tack immediately after coming on the wind at the moment **you** choose. Free wind on the beat is almost as important as on the reaches.

Maynard: There always seems to be a bunch of boats coming back from windward in to the mark on a dead run when you have positioned yourself for a close reach in to the buoy. They steal your wind, and you find yourself outside a pack aiming to do each other down and worse off than you should be. Nevertheless aim for this position – you should be travelling faster than they are and by holding a reaching course you can get the safe leeward berth on the bunch.

Peter White: The same techniques apply to all reaches; clear wind and the inside overlap at the mark are the important factors.

Crebbin: The inside berth on this leg is on the weather side. Because of this a bunch of boats will tend to luff much further above the direct line to the buoy, and so it is possible to gain a great distance by going well to leeward of the pack and coming up for the mark at the very last minute. You must decide to go this way as you round the gybe mark; the decision will be dictated by the other boats around, though it is the only way for the last man of a bunch to go to attack. The leeward mark is most

important – to come clear of other boat's dirty wind after rounding is imperative for any success in the early stages of the next beat.

Above all, avoid getting involved in luffing matches on both the reaching legs.

Reg White: In a catamaran you have to aim for a good buoy rounding at the leeward mark. Quite often boats will be approaching on starboard. Having right of way at the mark is of no value, for the port tack boats can slow up as the starboard tack boat approaches and either sail round it as it gybes or sneak in between it and the mark as it endeavours to go through its manoeuvre. Whatever happens, the starboard tacker will lose about five or six lengths.

Batt: If there are a lot of boats about it is worth hoisting out a bit to windward immediately after the gybe. This avoids being pushed up into 'the great circle' course.

Oakeley: Remember that the wind is likely to veer throughout the day and therefore this leg should be sailed to windward of the rhumb line, since the veer will bring the wind further ahead all the way down the leg. If the wind is blowing really hard, the spinnaker should be kept up after the gybe and, if necessary, the boat should be headed to leeward of the rhumb line, taking it down only when the angle to the mark gives a fine enough reach to keep planing at maximum speed.

Pattisson: The right way is of course a straight line, though this is only possible for the leader or if there is clear wind. If several boats are about, get well out to weather quickly and stay there to get the inside overlap at the mark. If you are behind several boats, go to leeward, especially if they are known to luff. The lighter the wind, the more important it is to stick near to the rhumb line.

With marks to port, how do you plan the reaches if the wind veers as much as 25 degrees while the first beat is still in progress?

Batt: If it veers a great deal, the stream of boats approaching the weather mark on the port tack lay-line will interfere with the straight line course to the gybe mark. Since the first reach has got broader there is great danger of being smothered by a bunch of boats going to weather. It still pays to get well down to leeward even though the reach has become broader, but not so far as to be jeopardized if the wind swings back. In the second, finer reach it is even more important to protect the weather side, for if the wind veered even more most of the boats to leeward would have trouble in making the mark on the one tack.

Pattisson: In close company with several other boats and a really big veer, it pays to gybe immediately after rounding the weather mark in order to get clear wind on the first reach. If the veer is not too great it is better to stay on the rhumb line whenever possible. The second reach is best attacked by going high early and bearing off to hoist the spinnaker.

Bruce: With a big veer it is almost certain that 90 per cent of the fleet will sail the first reach too high. It is therefore best to plan to sail that reach low immediately after rounding the weather mark. Conversely, immediately after gybing at the wing mark I would hold up high.

McNamara: The basic rule is to keep a clear wind by easing the minimum amount to windward. Going too far necessitates running to the gybe

mark, but that is better than having a pack of boats passing in clear air to windward while wallowing in their dirty wind and wash.

Jobbins: So much depends on the wind and the waves, but it is essential to keep clear air.

Oakeley: What the other competitors are doing is important but, generally speaking, with a persistently veering wind I would keep as far to leeward on the first reach as allowed.

Reg White: A big veer turns the first reach into a downwind tacking leg for catamarans. The aim, therefore, is to come into the gybe mark on port tack heading high on the second reach to allow for a further veer.

Warren: Five or ten degrees make little difference, but with slightly more it is imperative to go high on the second reach. If the veer becomes extreme I would take down the spinnaker at the gybe mark and close reach high on the second leg, setting the spinnaker again only if the veer did not persist.

Eyre: If the veer appeared to be continuing I would sail a leeward curve on the first reach and a windward curve on the second, no matter how strong the wind was.

Maynard: There is a danger that the entire fleet will sail too high a course on the first reach, especially if visibility is not very good. If helmsmen are using their compasses intelligently, this should not be a problem. The broader the first reach has become, the more it will pay to attack to leeward rather than to windward. If the veer is only temporary and is expected to swing back again then it will benefit those boats to windward first. On the second

Rodney Pattisson and Mike Brooke out ahead and keeping their wind clear from the Polish boat astern. The Poles should have made an attacking move by hardening up and sitting firmly on Pattisson's wind.

reach a windward course will be more favourable than normal, and an extreme veer will make any attack to leeward difficult.

Crebbin: The important thing is to locate the gybe mark so as to make sure that you are travelling in the right direction. If the veer is likely to continue the leeward course is the best on the first reach. On the second, it might be worth taking the spinnaker down before gybing, but if you are genuinely doubtful about this, keep it up, use it on the second reach and come back in towards the leeward mark without it.

Peter White: Because of its very large spinnaker, reaching in a *505* needs a slightly different technique. If you are uncertain whether the spinnaker could be carried, hoist it first and take it down if you realize you cannot make the mark with it set.

With a backing wind, how do you plan the reaches?

Eyre: In a continuing change, I would sail to windward on the first reach and a straight course, or slightly to windward, on the second, anticipating an approach on starboard gybe at the leeward mark with an inside berth.

Maynard: If the wind has backed it would probably pay to luff high on the first reach to take any boats that have not noticed the change and are sailing their normal reaching course. A shift of 5 to 10 degrees is not very significant, but more means that a windward course to the gybe mark is imperative, especially if the wind continues to back. If the wind is likely to veer again a rhumb line course is indicated on the second reach, but if the back continues a leeward course must be taken.

Oakeley: If I am at the head of the fleet on the first reach, I tend to sail high without the spinnaker, bearing away to set it into the gybe mark. At the back of the fleet I would hoist early, taking the spinnaker down to reach fast in to the gybe mark. With big shifts in the wind the tactics you adopt depend on where you are in the fleet.

Crebbin: The same principles apply as in a veering wind. If the next leg is nearly a run it often pays not to gybe at the wing mark but to go on, on starboard gybe, gybing later. That manoeuvre gained me fourteen places on one leg at Weymouth Olympic Week in 1975, a race I eventually won.

Peter White: On the first reach I would go low early in anticipation of the wind veering back to its median direction, although in *505s* a straight-line course is usually ideal.

Reg White: On the first reach, steer to leeward of the gybe mark and take advantage of a veer back to luff the boat and maintain maximum speed. The second reach becomes a downwind leg, and it is important to arrive at the leeward mark on the right gybe to start the next beat.

Warren: The more the wind backs, the more I delay setting the spinnaker on the first reach until I am certain that I can lay the gybe mark with it set. It is also more difficult to stay sufficiently to leeward on the second reach.

Jobbins: You have to allow for the wind to swing back, unless the forecast is that the wind will continue to go that way, and that is rare.

McNamara: The more the wind backs, the keener I am to sail a straight line on the first reach. If it is below planing speeds the boat behind must break through your quarter wave before it takes any wind from your sails.

Bruce: Go high on the first reach unless it is possible to sail a straight course without interference; sail a leeward circle on the second reach.

Batt: The tighter the first reach, the more difficult it is to sail a leeward course and the harder it is to be on the inside of the gybe. If the backing is extreme, a leeward course might pay off on the second reach and so being outside at the gybe might not be disastrous.

Pattisson: Go high early on the first reach and then hoist the spinnaker. On the second reach gybe immediately if necessary to keep your wind clear, unless the wind has backed 25 degrees or more when it may pay to hold on starboard gybe for 100 yards to get clear wind.

What factors affect the planning of the run? How do you approach the leeward mark?

Pattisson: I keep my wind clear and gybe on windshifts of 5 degrees or more. Close to other boats, I will manoeuvre regardless of gybe for an overlap at the leeward mark; otherwise I plan to arrive at the mark without having to gybe in rounding.

Warren: In a boat in which the spinnaker is not kept in a chute, planning the run is to some extent dictated by which gybe it was taken down on. Once it is up, the compass bearing to the mark controls which is the correct gybe.

Jobbins: In front I cover the chasing bunch: behind I go away from the leaders, get clear wind and attack from the flank.

Reg White: In a *Tornado* the right choice of tack downwind is all

The start of the run and while most of the Soling fleet at CORK 74 favour the starboard tack, the American boat on the left has decided to go off on port. Only a veering wind will help him.

important. The compass is your guide, and you must know how close to the rhumb line you can steer on either tack. Gybe on the heading shifts and use the freers to advantage. At the lee mark it is best to approach on port tack so that rounding is a simple manoeuvre.

McNamara: I choose the gybe that takes me nearest the mark, trying not to bear away on to a dead run for the buoy, particularly below displacement speed where tacking downwind is essential. If the speed is up to marginal planing, the dead run becomes less effective, and as the wind increases once again tacking downwind becomes the best plan, so that a gybe at the mark is not necessary.

Eyre: Always plan to run the shortest distance between the marks. Tide and wind strengths must be considered if one side or the other of the straight route is favoured. If a bunch of boats is approaching the leeward mark, I opt for the inside berth on starboard gybe; in that way I can control the manoeuvres of the rest of the fleet.

Batt: How you plan the run should be governed by the other boats nearby. In an *OK* it does not pay to tack downwind, except on the windshifts. It is best to be on the 'inside' of the slight circle and to stay clear of the boats behind. I gybe well before the mark so that I can get a smooth rounding, starting wide and aiming to pass the buoy just as I reach the close-hauled course. If, however, other boats are about, it is best to be with the inside berth at the mark, even if you are forced to gybe close to the buoy.

Peter White: Try to avoid a multitude of gybes. Consider the effect of the tides; if there is a tide gradient it is best to run with the strongest tide pushing you to weather.

Maynard: Running in a *Finn* and pumping the mainsheet are synonymous. Because there is no spinnaker there is no benefit in tacking downwind, and it is therefore better to utilize the waves, however small they may be, to get the best speed. The trick is to work to leeward down the waves, and then luff back fast to get the next one. Surfing down a large wave in a *Finn* by the lee requires great confidence and skill, but it really does pay handsome dividends. Keep an eagle eye behind you, to ensure clear wind for as far back as possible. It can be costly to go out all the way to windward to get clear wind; in this case it will probably pay to sail well by the lee with the boom out beyond the square for a short while to get clear wind down to leeward.

In large fleets, boats fanning into the leeward mark will slow those in front and cause a big pile-up. Do not get caught up in one of these 'rafts', but make for the inside position. You may have to slow up to get it, but you will lose less than if you are caught to leeward in a welter of dirty wind at the start of the next beat.

Bruce: I don't plan the run beforehand but concentrate on keeping clear wind, gybing as often as necessary. It does not pay to tack a *Laser* downwind. Like any other single-sailed boat, the *Laser* is best sailed slightly by the lee with a heel to windward. I try to come in to the leeward mark at least two boat lengths wide and at 90 degrees to the wind.

The start of the first reach in 30–35 knots of wind. Willi Kuhweide of Germany decides to sail high without setting his spinnaker for a while, to give him a fast and safe ride to the gybe mark after he has hoisted it. He will be restricted in his manoeuvres by a boat immediately to leeward. Note that the spinnaker pole is already hoisted. A little extra effort by the crew sitting out as far as possible would help at this time.

This gives the speed required to sail round any boat that has come in right on the buoy and has to spin to a close-hauled course if he has an overlap. It also gives the control and manoeuvrability required to harden up inside this same boat if he is ahead.

Crebbin: Wind streaks are very important on the run, as you can stay in them longer than on any other leg of the course and windshifts are the controlling factor for the correct gybe. How one approaches the leeward mark in a boat without a spinnaker chute depends on whether or not there is another triangle to do. If there are another two reaches to do, it is better to take the spinnaker down on the port side (when on starboard gybe) so that it is ready to hoist to leeward after rounding the weather mark (always assuming a port-hand course). Dropping the spinnaker on the correct side becomes more important as the wind increases.

Oakeley: The running leg must be planned on the previous windward leg, mainly so as to work out which will be the major gybe. Never round the weather mark viciously; this kills boatspeed. If you are staying on the same gybe it is worth holding on a reach for a few lengths to build up speed and to get clear wind from the boats astern. On approaching the leeward mark start to run in wide so that you approach the buoy on a reach, enabling you to get the spinnaker down early without losing speed and to round up efficiently on the wind, thus giving away the minimum amount at the mark.

How do you plan the start, taking into account line bias, numbers of competitors and even bad race committees?

Crebbin: The first criterion is

whether a particular side of the first beat is best. It is often worth starting at the 'wrong' end of a biased line so as to get to the best side of the beat first. Measure the compass bearing of the start line by sighting from a point some way from the pin buoy to the flagstaff on the committee boat, then, from the middle of the line, sight the windward mark and take its bearing. Be aggressive at the start, particularly in a large and competitive fleet. Your aim is to be just behind the line and sailing flat out when the gun goes, if possible in the pole position. If a lot of top helmsmen are about, it is not easy to get the pole position, and it is best sacrificed to gain clear space in which to manoeuvre. A series winner will always start in this manner rather than go for the pole position and get it four times out of six. In a starboard-biased start in particular there will be a lot of bunching at the weather end, and starting just to leeward of this bunch will not bring too much loss. There is never quite so much bunching at the pin end on a port-biased line, but then there is never any space to leeward to bear off and get the boat footing fast. A one- or five-minute rule does tend to restrict starting manoeuvres and if it means disqualification to be over early the fleet tends to become line shy.

Gate starts are easier with big fleets (at least for the committee). Where you should start in the gate depends entirely on which side of the course is favoured. Aim for the gate boat's stern with at least half a boat's length clear to leeward. If you are pathfinder and for some reason it is obvious that early starters are favoured, do not be afraid to throw the start. There is no reason why you should lose the championship or series. Halfway down the gate, let all

128

your sails go. You cannot be disqualified and the race will be restarted.

Oakeley: To make a good start at
the port end of the line, come in
towards the bunch heading down the
line with a couple of minutes to go on
port tack. Then tack immediately
underneath the leader of the bunch and
from that position you will control the
start. To start well at the other end of the
line, it is often best to come in three or
four seconds late, for the majority of
those aiming for that place will have
come in too soon and will have drifted
off to leeward. If the right-hand side of
the course is favoured, it does not
matter if one boat is dead in front, as
you will be able to dictate when anyone
can tack.

Bruce: This is the most important
single part of a *Laser* race, and very few
competitors are mentally,
psychologically or physically warmed
up by the time the starting-gun goes.
Only those with at least twenty
minutes' hard sailing under their belt
will be ready for the start. An accurate
bearing of the starting line must be
obtained by sighting along the line from
beyond the pin end to the committee
boat's flagstaff. Then read the mean
wind direction and judge which is the
biased end. Next, assess which side of
the course is favoured and then start
according to the chart (p. 130). I never
go for the pin end of the line, especially
in big fleets. At the start it is essential to
be moving fast, preferably in the centre
area of the line, where there always
tends to be a sag. There are also fewer
boats here, and one can usually tack
into clear air immediately. It also helps
to take a transit on the line, forward
preferably but backward if necessary.
From behind the committee boat sight
along its stern to the pin buoy and find a

shore feature as a transit. If this is
impossible, take a backward transit by
sighting from the pin buoy to the stern
of the committee boat and look for a
shore feature there as a transit. Always
use the stern of the committee boat, for
it gives half a boat's length safety factor.
Once started, never sail in dirty wind.
Tack, tack, and tack again, just so long
as you keep moving in clear air.

Jobbins: Starting needs quick
thinking and readiness to alter plans at
the last minute.

Eyre: I always time my approach
with a dummy run from a known
position, so that I contrive to arrive on
the line travelling fast. If there is a
starboard bias I tend to go about a third
of the way down the line from the
committee boat in order to get clear
wind, but if there is a port bias I cannot
stop myself from having a go at the pole
position.

Peter White: Under no
circumstances would I go for the pin
end in a big fleet.

Batt: The obvious essentials are a
clear wind at the right end of the line
and ability to tack at will. I try to start
away from the bunch, if possible to
leeward of it.

McNamara: It is a waste of time
to be in the second or third rank. In a big
fleet get out early and stake your claim
to the piece of the starting line you
want. *Enterprises* usually have gate
starts which, if there is no major
windshift during the starting period, are
the best way to control the start of a big
championship fleet. I never risk a really
early start, for it is impossible to know
exactly when the starting buoy will be
dropped after the pathfinder has
started. I then work to put a lee bow on
the boat to windward so that I can tack
if I wish.

129

Pattisson: In a small fleet I go for the pole position on a biased line every time. In a large fleet with a marginal bias I attempt to start near the middle of the line with my wind clear, having made sure of a transit beforehand. I try to avoid starting to weather of anyone who I know points high. If there is a large bias and a large fleet, I know that there will be a big bunch of boats going for the favoured place and I start just to their unbiased side in clear wind.

Reg White: Where to start depends entirely on where you want to go on the beat. The bias on a line is rarely so bad, so it pays to start on the 'wrong' end of the line for the favoured side of the course.

Warren: I examine the major opposition and try to start away from them, leaving a good gap to leeward.

Maynard: Very often it is all important to be among the first to reach a particular side of the windward leg. This will decide which end of the line to start. At the starboard side of the course, it may pay to be a few seconds late at the committee boat with the right to tack on to port as soon as the anchor chain is cleared. If a bad race committee is likely to let a fleet go although many were over the line, there is only one way to go – with the fleet.

		Favoured side of course	Start Position	Course of Action
1.	*'Pin' heavily favoured* (Reverse all these for "Boat" instead of "Pin")	(a) Lefthand – port	25% from pin	Sail hard and free – tack only if absolutely necessary. Get back on starboard as soon as possible.
		(b) Neither	30% from pin	Tack or not, according to shift*.
		(c) Righthand – starboard	50% from pin	Tack as soon as possible.
2.	*'Pin' slightly favoured*	(a) Lefthand	30% from pin	Sail hard and fast – tack only if absolutely necessary. Return to starboard as soon as possible.
		(b) Neither	30% from pin	Tack or not, according to shift.
		(c) Righthand	30% from boat	Tack as soon as possible.
3.	*Neither end favoured*	(a) Left	30% from pin	Tack only if badly headed; return to starboard after consolidating position.
		(b) Neither	50% from pin	Play shifts.
		(c) Right	30% from boat	Tack to right in first header; work towards right.

*One of the things which should have been thoroughly observed during the warm-up period is your high and low point of sailing on the wind.

Chapter 15
Attacking tactics

Attacking tactics consist of using changing wind and other conditions to gain advantages over other competitors, rather than simply to get to the next mark in the shortest time, and also of encouraging a rival ahead to make a mistake. The questions put to the Champions covered the principal situations in which attacking tactics might be used.

You have started two-thirds of the way down the line, and after a few minutes there is a 10-degree header. How do you get clear on to port? How much of a shift is necessary for you to tack at this stage? And how much are you prepared to give away to get clear?

Pattisson: If the line bias were less than 10 degrees on the starboard side and my windward performance equal to or better than the rest, I would tack and find I had cleared all the other boats; but I would be prepared to give away as much as three boat lengths at this stage to take advantage of the shift. If the line were true I would tack on anything more than 5 degrees at this stage.

Warren: With any luck the header comes to put you in front of those who were on your weather side. But if not you must wait your turn and then tack or go astern of the next boat in line. Anything less than 10 degrees is not enough at this stage but I might give away a good deal to get clear, going under as many as twenty boats if I though it was the correct thing to do.

Maynard: Whether one can tack across the fleet on port after a header soon after the start depends on the bias of the line and its length. If there were

that kind of header for a boat two-thirds down from the starboard end of a longish line with a 15-degree starboard bias, there's no chance of being able to tack on to port to clear the fleet as the boats further to windward will still be ahead. Assuming that there is no bias on the line there is a better chance of tacking and clearing those previously to weather. A 10-degree header is not large but with no bias on the line it would give the boats at the port end a distinct advantage. The boat that started close to the pin-end mark with reasonable boatspeed should be able to tack to clear the fleet once the heading shift is established throughout the fleet. The leeward boat will experience the shift first but it may take a minute or two before the whole fleet is affected. A boat two-thirds down the line should also have an advantage over the remaining boats to windward.

As the wind heads the back-winding effect on all starboard boats will be increased, so it is important to be able to tack quickly before backwinding causes loss of distance. If you can clear the boat immediately on your starboard side, you should tack at once. Remember that the boat immediately to windward is affected by your backwind, so it may pay to hang on for a short time until he drops back a little because of this, but boats to leeward will have begun to tack and the last place that you want to be is in their dirty wind. If you cannot cross the first two boats to windward it is worth looking for a gap behind them where you can cross the rest of the fleet. As to the degree of shift necessary to tack, this depends whether it is an oscillating wind or not, because it is most important to stay in phase with the oscillations. The larger the shift the more important it is to stay in phase. If the header is the result of a long progressive swing, it would be wise to hang on to the starboard tack for as long as is necessary to take full advantage of this type of shift.

Batt: By forcing up under the lee bow of the boat immediately on your weather side you should be able to force him to tack. Then there will be enough room for you to clear the rest of the fleet. I don't like going behind anyone if I am on the port side of the course at this stage. Fifteen degrees would mean that I would most certainly tack, but a lot would depend on the wind strength. If I wanted to get out to the right-hand side of the course I would go on 10 degrees, but for me the only way up the windward lee is in clear air.

Peter White: In general it's a good tactic to tack on to port as soon as possible after the start. If I could do that and clear most of the boats originally upwind, then it could be worth giving away a length or two to make space to do so. If possible it is worth going straight on to port tack without immediate interference from other boats, even if there has not been a 10-degree header.

McNamara: If I can tack I do so even if I have to go behind the boat immediately to windward, but it's horrible if he tacks at that moment, too. If I can't tack I squeeze to lee bow those stopping me, even to the point of slowing up a bit to do so. If the wind shifts enough to bring me down on the boat in front and to leeward, I always want to tack. How much I am prepared to give away depends upon the permanence of the shift. If it is varying a lot I might go and bear away a great deal so that I can capitalize on the next

starboard freeing shift. If it's permanent I don't mind sailing into the header for some time.

Reg White: It's not worth tacking in a catamaran with less than a 10-degree wind shift. With 15 degrees, on the other hand, it would certainly be worthwhile giving something away to get on to port tack. But when the wind heads by 10 degrees it is best to sail the boat much freer and gain distance by boatspeed to give yourself enough room to tack if the shift heads further.

Jobbins: There has to be a great deal of wind before I will get into any close-quarter battles with a bunch of starboard tackers if I'm on port tack. If possible I will tack on any shift of 10 degrees or more as soon as possible, but if I had enough speed to effect a lee bow on the boat immediately to windward I would do so and make him tack first.

Bruce: Tack if at all possible. With a 5-degree shift it's questionable, with a 10-degree one it's essential, and with 15 degrees I would bear off first if necessary and dip as many sterns as necessary. If the shift is even more I would lee bow the nearest boat and try to force a mass movement.

Oakeley: If there were a 10-degree header the whole *Soling* fleet would go about on to port. A shift of 3 to 5 degrees is enough to tack on in a close-winded boat, but with a trapeze dinghy 7 degrees is minimal. If the wind is going to swing back again I would be prepared to dive under several sterns to get to the other side of the course.

Reg White (218) is just to weather of Niel Coster (123). This is a crucial time for White, who is affected by the backwind off Coster's sails. He must anticipate every gust. If he can edge another 6 feet forward, relative to Coster, he will begin to take the other's wind and soon go ahead. On the other hand, if he falls off to leeward at all, or if Coster can squeeze up, White is in danger.

Eyre: It depends entirely on whether the shift is permanent or temporary. If it is permanent I would wait until I could clear everyone to windward, if it is only temporary I would tack immediately and dip a few sterns to get to the right side of the course.

Crebbin: If you have made a good start you should only have to duck a few boats to clear across to the other side of the course. Don't go unless it costs you very little, because if you have to go under the sterns of most of the fleet you will lose all the advantage of the windshift. If you are undecided it's often worthwhile tacking and ducking a few to gauge how things are going. If it doesn't look good, tack back again. Just after the start you should certainly be taking a long-term view, and clear wind is more important than one windshift.

You are being covered hard on the windward leg and you know that on this point you are faster than the boat in front. How do you get free?

Eyre: With the *Moth's* rapid acceleration there are many different possibilities. The most effective is to break clear to leeward by bearing off, even if it means close-reaching to do so. Unless the leading boat follows suit clear wind is quickly reached, and from then on you have to stay on the same tack until you can make two tacks to a lee bow position. If one can point significantly higher than the boat ahead it is simple to induce a tacking battle to climb out to windward.

McNamara: Tack and tack again, then bear away when close and try to drive through to leeward, being careful not to get dragged to the wrong side of the course or so far one way that you cannot tack to get free.

Jobbins: If I can sail past with sheer power and boatspeed I'll probably try breaking his cover with a dummy tack. On the last beat this situation can be one of the most exciting parts of the race, especially when there's a lot of wind and you are lying second.

Peter White: I throw in a few quick tacks until I can shake off the cover, rather than footing off and ending up a long way to one side of the course.

Batt: I dictate the tacks with the aim of forcing him into a wrong move, tacking him into a big wave for instance. Anything like a double tack is worth a try, especially if it upsets the covering boat. At some point there will be a chance to drive off into clear air. It pays to be irregular so that the covering boat has to watch all the time.

Crebbin: Avoid letting the boat in front sit on you on the same tack. You should be practised enough at tacking in any weather to be able to get on a different tack. Then keep tacking on the shifts and you will make better use of them. If the two of you are well clear tacking duels can be great fun. I try never to be beaten in a tacking duel, which is the first essential for shaking off a close cover. Team-racing experience counts enormously for that. It is even worth considering dummy tacks, but these are dangerous in high-performance boats.

Oakeley: It's only possible for someone to give dirty wind on one tack. If you go about, you will find that he is too far back to affect you. This is the tack on which I try to break through.

Bruce: With my weight I will always sail free and attempt to drive through to leeward.

Reg White: In a catamaran you

134

have to wait for the moment to tack so that you do not lose too much distance over the other competitors when you are covered hard. I always try to drive through to leeward, preferably when on port tack, so that when I have got well clear I can come about on to starboard and have right of way.

Maynard: If you are a faster tacker than the covering boat, initiate a tacking duel. Once the leading boat realizes that you are winning he will probably break it off. Early on it may pay to try to fool the leader with a false tack, but good helmsmen are rarely taken in by this and you are more likely to lose distance than gain any advantage. If the wind is oscillating you can try sailing the leader into the headers. Because he is ahead and to windward he will reach them first. If you sail well into the header before you tack you will gain more from each shift than the leader. It is a common mistake for attacking skippers to tack the moment they feel the header, with the result that they do not get into the true wind and the defending boat gets the better of the shift.

Another tactic is deliberately to sail the wrong way; this will make the defending skipper feel very uneasy, especially if there are other boats not too far behind. In this situation he might well tack away to follow the best course. Once you can clear your wind from the leader, tack yourself and attack his weather. If you are on the last leg there will be other boats coming down on the run. By carefully judging your tacks you might be able to sail the leader into a bunch of running boats which will either slow him down or prevent him from tacking to cover.

Warren: I would sail free, driving through to leeward and pointing out

again once I had clear wind.

Pattisson: If we were well clear of all the other boats in the fleet I would do anything to get my wind clear; I find that continuous tacking, dummy tacks and bearing off are the three best ways to break the cover. You have to take more care if you are close to other good boats. In those cases I would use the windshifts or try to make the leader tack into an inconvenient place. More likely, though, I would bear off to clear my wind.

You are on the favoured port tack with a row of boats coming across on starboard. You just cannot cross the leader. How many boats would you dip the sterns of, or would you tack to get a lee bow position on the leader?

Maynard: This is only likely to happen on the first leg, when boats are still fairly close together. If it is just after the start, it would probably pay to duck under four or five sterns to be sure of getting clear air on the correct tack. You are only likely to meet larger groups of starboard tacking boats immediately after the start. If the windward plan makes it imperative to get over to the starboard side of the course it will often pay to duck under quite a number of sterns. If you do this very soon after the start you will not lose very much distance, especially if you can achieve clear wind as soon as you have crossed under them all. If the situation arose some way up the beat, or on the second round, it would probably not pay to give away four boat lengths or more in order to stay on the port tack, unless you were expecting to gain a very large amount from wind or current on the right-hand side of the course. In most cases it is far better to tack underneath a line of boats and tack back when they tack to take advantage of the shift.

Bruce: I would only duck under a row of boats if they were staggered. If they were in line astern the ones behind the leader must be stupid, so I would tack to force a lee bow situation on the first boat; very shortly, therefore, I would be able to tack back on to port. Because the *Laser* tacks very quickly it is better not to give ground away by bearing off under the sterns of boats unless it is essential to get to the other side of the course.

Crebbin: If you are only just failing to cross, you should be able to tack and lee bow the leader, in which case it will not be long before you can tack back, if the port tack is still favourable. You have to gauge just how important it is to stay on the favourable tack. It's very rarely important enough to lose four boat lengths, let alone six or eight. In a high-performance boat in heavy weather you are much more likely

to bear off; but if you are in danger of getting backwind from the boats to leeward, the best solution may be to slow the boat and stay on the same tack, in the same line.

Warren: If I thought it was the right thing to do I would duck under any number of boats, though what they would all be doing on the wrong tack I don't know. I would tack back on to starboard if two of them tacked on my wind or if I thought the wind was going round to favour the port tack even more later.

Pattisson: If I know I can out-point the leader, I will tack just ahead and to leeward. If I cannot out-point him and the port tack is notably favoured I would go under as many as

The helmsman of Finn 19 at the 1972 Olympics is making a late effort at the leeward mark. He has no rights over 23 but will round the mark immediately astern of him and in a better position than 10, who is likely to come out of this rounding behind 16.

four boats. Tacking underneath six would help to separate them so that I would quickly be in a position to tack back onto port and get into clear air.

Reg White: If the port tack is really worthwhile I would always duck under three or four boats rather than lose ground in tacking – in a catamaran this can be as much as three or four lengths; in this way I would take advantage of the next windshift, which favours those on the right-hand side of the course.

Oakeley: In a trapeze boat I would duck the sterns of up to four boats, but in a *Soling* I would tack to leeward of the leader of two or more boats.

Batt: If I wanted to be safe, a close lee bow on the first boat would keep me in touch with that bunch, maybe forcing a few to tack away. If I were expecting a big starboard lift I would go behind four boats to put as much distance between myself and the opposition as I could before the shift occurred. Just how near I was to the extreme edge of the course would be a big factor in determining whether or not I tacked; one doesn't want to be forced to the lay-line too early.

Peter White: A lot depends on the proximity of the windward mark. If it is some way distant it is probably worth going under three or four boats. Generally, by dipping a couple of boats you build up enough speed to shoot across in front of the third. Close to the mark I would tack under the leader to gain a safe leeward position on him.

Jobbins: So much depends on the wind and sea conditions. In a reasonable breeze and flat water I would tack underneath a line of boats to get a lee bow on the leader. If there is a lot of sea running I would be prepared to go under six or eight, because once

clear you can sort out your own boatspeed unhindered, getting the best of the shift back and attacking the bunch as they come towards you on port tack.

Eyre: I would not want to lose more than one boat's length of windward position in order to pass under any number of boats on starboard tack.

McNamara: I would tack as close as possible to the leader and really squeeze hard to put him behind me so that I could get back on to the port tack quickly. The snag is that if they all tack I would be lee bowed. In windy weather I would bear away and use the speed for a good luff around the last stern of up to five boats; more and I am back to the lee bow attack.

How effective do you consider the lee bow to be?

McNamara: Very much so, it's a real killer because the windward boat cannot luff to get out of it. Should it do so it loses speed altogether. The only way out is to tack immediately.

Crebbin: I agree; they're effective partly because they have a great psychological influence. The helmsman to weather is always worrying whether he is being slowed by a lee bow and invariably sails his boat badly. With a trapeze boat it is not possible to tack as close in a blow and so it is therefore less effective. Personally, I much prefer being to leeward than to weather when attacking.

Pattisson: The lee bow effect works on boats up to one and a half lengths to windward and five lengths astern.

Bruce: In a *Laser*, without the additional effect of the slot, you are particularly vulnerable to a lee-bow tack. Because of its manoeuvrability the

Laser's tactics revolve around lee bow tacking.

Oakeley: The bigger the boat, the more effective the lee bow.

Jobbins: It appears to work best in trapezing winds, but psychologically it is very effective in light airs.

Batt: It's very, very effective. When a boat is tacked quickly and accurately the windward boat doesn't have a chance. If it tries to luff away it loses speed, and its only real alternative is to tack off.

Peter White: Since I rely on pointing high when sailing to windward, I find the lee bow a good tactic. I can often tack eight lengths to leeward of most people in a fleet and work up to a lee bow position in most wind strengths.

Reg White: It is a very difficult tactic to exploit with a catamaran because of the slow tacking. It often happens that the boat you are trying to corner in this way bears off under you as you tack and applies the lee bow to you. It is only really effective when tacking for the windward mark on the lay-line when it is essential to squeeze out the boats behind.

Warren: It's most effective in Force 2 and least effective in Force 6.

Eyre: It's effective as long as the boat to windward cannot point higher than you. In a development class like the *Moth* the pointing abilities of boats vary considerably, and it's sometimes possible for a really close-winded boat to claw its way out of a lee bow situation.

Maynard: It can be a very effective attacking weapon in a *Finn,* which can be tacked very quickly under certain conditions. In international fleets, however, it is not practised a great deal because of the protest risks

involved. With a *Finn* the close lee bow tack can only be effectively carried out in light to medium conditions on flat water. In very light or very strong winds too much way is lost and the windward boat will tramp over the top of the lee bow tacker.

How safe do you think it is to tack as close as is necessary if the lee bow is to be effective, bearing in mind that the onus of proof is on you if a protest is made?

Warren: It depends which country you're racing in. In Britain you can tack very close, well within one boat's length, and this is accepted as normal. In Europe they get very excited if you go this close, and I think this is because, in general, they have not raced small dinghies and do not accept dinghy ways.

Peter White: Despite my team-racing background I don't think it necessary to tack very close to impose the lee bow effect. I work up from a position well to leeward. It saves all the hassles associated with tacking too close.

Maynard: For the lee bow tack to be effective, it must be carried out very close to the other boat. If there is a collision the tacking boat's chances at a protest meeting will not be very good – the windward boat does not have to start to alter course until the leeward boat's tack is completed. The windward boat must have reasonable opportunity to keep clear. If you are unsure of how your opponent will react to a close lee bow tack, it's best not to try it on.

Batt: I don't think it is necessary to tack at all in front of a boat. In any case

John Dawson-Edwards in K 342 should tack to clear his wind rather than follow the two immediately ahead. The right-hand side of the course is favoured this day, but he has no chance of passing the boats ahead from his present position.

it's dangerous. If you tack to leeward there is no reason for the windward boat to alter course, at least not until the full effect of your lee bow is felt.

Eyre: I believe the lee bow is effective within two boat lengths and, with the *Moth's* acceleration, this is not risky. There is no need to go close enough for a collision to take place.

Reg White: Within a half length to leeward and three clear ahead is about the right timing for the tack. By the time your tack is completed your opponent should be within one boat's length of your transom, in a catamaran.

Oakeley: It depends entirely on the type of boat you're sailing. With a *Soling* it is not necessary to tack very close. With a trapeze boat it helps to tack as close as you can because even if the weather boat is going faster it is not possible for him to luff up enough to get past the trapeze man.

Jobbins: I find that the top sailors try hard to stay out of this sort of trouble. I would never push my luck and tack closer than half a length to leeward.

Bruce: Because of the *Laser's* manoeuvrability the lee bow tack can be very close and still be very safe.

Pattisson: I would go as close as half a boat's length to leeward of another, and no less. If tacking directly ahead I would allow two and a half lengths: it is just too risky to go closer in case you foul the tack.

McNamara: It depends upon wave conditions, but I reckon to be able to tack within a boat's length so that when I finish my tack he is at least 5 feet away. I would always tack just to leeward so that the boat with right of way could sail past to windward without hitting me and without altering course. Then I'd bring the boat very

upright, heeling slightly to windward if anything, and squeeze.

Crebbin: Tacking close enough in light weather shouldn't be a problem. In heavier weather the *470* is sailed faster slightly free; therefore one has to tack safely to leeward and in front and begin the squeeze sailing slightly more slowly, but establishing the lee bow after the tack. If the weather boat also squeezes up I then free off and have gained a lot before he has realized that he can bear off again.

What other attacking moves do you consider important on a windward leg?

Bruce: If you are being covered by an opponent it is important to try to tack so that, if he tacks to cover, he will be disturbed by a third boat. In the absence of other boats, tacking in a lifting breeze when you are covered invariably closes the gap, and your competitor will find it extremely difficult to defend himself.

Crebbin: Psychology plays an enormous part. Whenever another helmsman looks at you it's as well to luff a little so that he believes that you are pointing higher than you actually are. Conversely, if in a stronger breeze he is in a position from which he can't really see how you are pointing, free off a bit when he looks and really pick up speed. This can be very disconcerting. Keep sailing on the opposite tack if the wind is steady and your opponent is in front; this will make him look backwards and erode his concentration.

McNamara: I'm in favour of loosely covering the man immediately behind so that he feels he not only has to sail faster but that he has to get past me and my wind shadow. If I'm behind I either try to tack to leeward so that if the helmsman wants to see me he has to lose concentration by looking underneath the boom, or else I tack way up on the leader's quarter so that the helmsman has to turn hard to see where I am.

Pattisson: When approaching the weather mark on the lay-line I bear off as a boat crosses astern. This ensures that its helmsman will tack late and thereby overstand the mark.

Oakeley: The best possible position for covering is dead ahead of your opponent. Not only can he see you all the time, which upsets him; it also gives him a considerable amount of disturbed air and allows you complete control over his manoeuvres.

Eyre: Sailing free to a clear wind position is without doubt the best attacking tactic in a *Moth*. Breaking cover with a false tack can be risky as the *Moth* stops quickly when brought head to wind.

Maynard: It's worthwhile attacking to windward when sailing on a lifting shift. By sailing fast and free you can sail over the top of a boat to leeward and give it dirty wind. The helmsman will then have to tack away and go on to the bad tack. If you are near the finish you can go with him and maintain your new-found cover. In oscillating winds, when trying to overtake an opponent who works the shifts correctly, wait for him to tack on a shift and then go on a little further so that you tack behind but upwind. Then sail flat out before the next shift, when you have to repeat the manoeuvre until you finally get through. If you are attacking another boat on the beat in shifty winds, ensure that you sail well into each shift. You can lose out badly by tacking below a lifted boat which you cannot cross simply because you yourself do not sail far enough into the

shift. It is often better to sail on behind a lifted boat and tack slightly to windward. Then, if the shift continues, you will get lifted above your opponent.

Peter White: It's possible to place oneself upwind of an opponent on the same tack so that you can see the opposition just ahead of your forestay. From there you can easily compare your performance with that of the boat ahead.

Batt: Sometimes it's worth encouraging an opponent up a wrong windshift or out into the tide, even though you may have the right of way, by shouting: 'Hold your course port boat, I'll go under you.'

Warren: Tacking dead ahead, about five lengths or so, is extremely effective. It puts the helmsman astern in a fix; first he will try to point out of it and fail, then he may try to sail free and off to leeward, and eventually he will decide he has to tack. But meanwhile he will have lost a lot of ground, more than if you had tacked right on his wind.

What do you consider the correct way of passing another boat on a reach?

Pattisson: If there is only one boat then I go well to weather. If there are several, then I go well to leeward.

Eyre: There is only one effective way – at close quarters to windward, though in order to avoid a luffing match you will have to go at least a couple of lengths to windward of your opponent. In a large fleet a clear leeward course often pays off, but it has to be a long way to leeward and it is a painful process.

Oakeley: It is difficult to pass a boat on a reach and only really possible immediately after rounding the previous mark, when the boat just ahead of you is either hoisting his spinnaker or gybing it; if you are quicker and better than him at this, you will pass him. One thing is certain though, you will never get through to leeward.

McNamara: Similar boatspeeds, large wave formations and vulnerability to luffing make it hard to pass to windward in an *Enterprise.* Passing to leeward is also difficult because of the boat's large sailarea; all the boat in front has to do is to keep you in his quarter wave and you are dead. You therefore have to go quite a long way to windward and wait for the boat in front to make a mistake. But never give up, keep the pressure up all the time.

Reg White: The correct way of passing another yacht on the reach is to weather. You must do this early, before your opponent is caught. You have to go up at exactly the same moment as he decides he wants to luff, keeping the gap between the two of you parallel.

You must anticipate his manoeuvre and beat him to it. Once he has dictated to you when he is going to luff, the game becomes a lead boat situation because you have driven up too close to him.

Warren: Go very high to start with and keep a good deal to weather of your opponent, so that he never feels that he can luff up that far. In addition, as you go by, he will think that not too much harm has been done to his wind.

Maynard: Either by attacking to windward from very close astern or from many boat lengths to windward. If you are coming close astern it is possible to play your opponent's stern wave and surf up very close behind. Make a few moves to leeward so that your opponent thinks you are going to

A perfectly timed start for H 11 who will control the boats to windward unless the wind frees on the starboard tack. He should be able to drive off fast to pull clear of GO 17 and will then be clear to tack across the fleet.

try to attack him that way, then, when you can catch a good wave or a strong gust, luff up hard, pump the sail and plane through his wind before he has much time to react. Alternatively you can pass some considerable distance to windward so as to dissuade your opponent from luffing. Trying to pass on a reach to leeward is next to impossible.

Jobbins: There is only one way. Wait until the boat in front is in the slowest part of the wave pattern and then turn on your own power by using your wave at exactly the right moment, pumping the sheets as you do so. The only other way is to go a long way to windward to avoid being luffed.

Batt: It depends on the reach. On close reaches, if I'm going fast I go very wide to windward. On a broad reach in surfing conditions passing to leeward becomes more practical, as wind shadow has relatively little effect and the waves more.

Peter White: After rounding the weather mark I get the crew to rig the spinnaker pole to force the leading boat into hoisting his spinnaker. Then I sail high without a spinnaker for a few boat lengths and rely on a quick hoist to break through to windward. Halfway down the reach I use the waves and the right gust to attack the leading boat's weather and try to stay far enough away from him to avoid a vicious luff.

Bruce: If you have enough power, you can get through on a close reach to leeward about two or three boat lengths away, as long as there is enough wind to plane. This only applies if you can utilize more power than your opponent to windward. On a broader reach, you have to go through to windward,

though it is essential to steer well clear. Do not slide up slowly, make a very definite move well to windward.

Crebbin: The quickest way to overtake, assuming your competitors take no defensive action, is to windward. On boats with spinnakers minor sail alterations bring enormous differences in speed, and so it is very important to keep the boat perfectly balanced. Concentrate on tricking the leading boat into a violent manoeuvre to try to stop you passing. It will slow a lot and then it is easy to get to 'mast abeam', particularly in stronger winds. The helmsman who has to look astern has trouble keeping his boat going at optimum speed.

How do you deal with people who are known to luff, sometimes to their own detriment?

Bruce: Shout a lot – and swear too.

Crebbin: These people set themselves up for the overtaking-to-leeward trick. They alter course violently to stop you passing to windward and virtually stop themselves. Look for a lack of co-ordination in your opponent's boat and attack accordingly. Never give up five places to gain this one, however; it's best to steer well clear of this type.

Reg White: Take a high course and sail round your opponent.

McNamara: I try to go to windward, and then, if I am luffed, I stay there, unless it gets out of proportion; then you have to slow your own boat and break off the challenge. Working the waves will often break into your opponent's wind, and then passing is easier.

Warren: Hope that I'm already

ahead by the time the reaches come.

Oakeley: Should an opponent always luff when you try to pass, it's often worthwhile slowing down and letting the next boat past you so that he gets involved and you can bear away out of it as they chase each other to the horizon.

Jobbins: Keep out of their way.

Batt: Give them a wide berth on the close reaches and go to leeward on the broader ones.

Pattisson: Try to aim to weather when they are not looking or drop the spinnaker and luff hard to weather out of their reach and hoist again quickly.

Eyre: In light winds I stay well to leeward and let someone else try to go through to weather to give me clear wind. In planing conditions I tempt him to luff and at the last minute dive hard for his lee.

The ultimate in gybe mark problems at pre-Olympic CORK 1975, and a time when the inside berth is essential. It even pays to slow up and cross the sterns of a line of boats to be second (on the inside) rather than try to pull out to leeward.

Peter White: Try not to get involved.

Maynard: It's often a good idea to talk to this type of helmsman as you approach, explaining that if he luffs he is going to lose even more places. I am afraid that middle-of-the-fleet skippers, as these invariably are, can often be intimidated on the water by a few sharp words from a top skipper. The incorrigible luffer is an uncommon phenomenon in good-quality fleets. Most good skippers take the view that if a faster boat is going through to windward it is best to let him through and lose the minimum distance over it.

Fisher: It is obvious that everyone of these champions is aware of the dangers of the inveterate luffer. A good defensive tactic might therefore be to put it about that you are one! It's not necessary to practice the habit all the time, but the occasional really vicious luff when a lot of people are watching and it doesn't matter where you finish in the fleet may bring you the reputation of being a luffer; you will then have little trouble in the future from boats trying to come past too close to windward.

Are there any other attacking tactics you consider important?

Batt: Simple covering on the run helps, as much by irritating the other helmsman as anything else. Anything that makes him steer unnecessarily or manoeuvre quickly and roughly can help to slow him down.

Crebbin: Confidence in the co-ordination and teamwork inside your own boat is the first requirement for attacking other boats. With this you will

be able to out-think your opponents. For example, on a run you can often overtake by covering and spinnaker gybing better, and with this confidence you will be in the best position to institute a duel of this sort.

Maynard: Many helmsmen have a habit of yelling 'starboard' at every opportunity of putting a port tack boat about. The port tacker should then put in a beautiful lee-bowing tack, forcing the starboard hailer to tack away, wondering what went wrong. If the starboard tacker knows that he is on the favoured tack he should encourage port tackers to keep going across his bow and out of harm's way by calling 'You're OK, keep going.' It would be a ruthless competitor who would then tack beneath him, and few competitors are ruthless enough with their tactics.

Jobbins: If you have a particular strength, let the others know about it; it's bound to upset the opposition when those particular conditions occur.

McNamara: The essential tactic is constant aggression. Never give up, and be patient.

Bruce: When behind, concentrate on boats several places ahead, not on those in the immediate vicinity. By watching those further up in the fleet you will be in a position to pick up a shift or a change faster than those around you. This is particularly true on the windward leg. On a reach, try to gain the attention of the competitor immediately in front of you; talk to him incessantly if necessary, and do everything to distract him.

Chapter 16
Defensive tactics

Once ahead, the problem is to stay ahead – and not necessarily only at the front of the fleet: in a series every place is valuable, and it could be critical to stay ahead of a particularly close rival, even though on that leg he may be noticeably faster. It is in defence that consolidation tactics take over; these aim to maintain the gain already made rather than to go out on a limb in the hope of making an even bigger gain, when, if anything goes wrong, many places will be lost.

How early in a race should defensive tactics be employed? Does the reasoning alter at any time during a series?

Maynard: Defensive tactics should be employed throughout the race to preserve gains that have been made. In the early stages they will be carried out against the whole fleet, whereas in the later stages they will be employed against individual boats. Good helmsmen often put in an early port tack after the start to take advantage of a shift or break into clear air on the starboard side of the course. If you find yourself ahead of or well up on the majority of the fleet, you should not continue to hang on a port tack if the rest of the fleet stays on starboard, no matter what your own convictions may be. Instead, tack back on to starboard and stay with the fleet. If the wind veers you will gain; if it backs, you will not lose out as much as if you had held on longer on port tack.

Similarly, if you make a perfect start on port and begin to draw away, don't continue too long, but tack on to port and join the main body of the fleet. If it is possible to cross the fleet on port

soon after the start, then tack back on to starboard as soon as the other side of the fleet is reached. In my experience, the majority decision of the fleet about the correct tack is more reliable than an individual's hunch. This does not mean, however, that if you are certain of the right way you have to follow the fleet. If you have some information or knowledge that the rest of the fleet does not have, then it is perfectly reasonable to follow your own course. I find you are most likely to have to make brilliant starts and take flyers when you do not have good boatspeed. Skippers who are going very fast usually adopt very conservative tactics and are therefore very safe.

Sometimes, at the end of a series, the surest way to win is to sail your nearest opponent into the middle of the fleet for a certain discard for him (and for you). You can only do this if you have a set of good and consistent results, but it enables you to play havoc with a competitor who already has a bad result in his score. Alternatively, you may have a small overall lead over the next man and have to finish in front of him in the last race to take home the silverware. In this case you have a match race on your hands and the way you tackle the start of such a race is vital, for it is then that you must get ahead of your rival.

Pattisson: It depends on the points situation, whether you are leading the series and have one or more principal rivals. If I am leading at the first mark, I adopt defensive tactics from then on, whether it is the first race of a series or the last. In the case of the normal seven-race series with six to count, I begin to defend against one boat after the fourth race; if there are more than one, I start only in the last two races of the series.

Peter White: I believe that you should defend as soon as you are in a position to do so. If, for instance, you make a good start and can cross the fleet, it is good defensive tactics to take the advantage then and there. Of course, one puts more accent on defence towards the end of a series that you are leading or in a race in which you are in front; but defence should form part of the total armoury.

Jobbins: I agree. All too often in a series you find yourself battling with the same boat, and it never pays to let that one past.

Reg White: You must attack until you are in front, then defend. There are some exceptions, however, and many a time I am content with second or third place as long as I am in front of my principal rival in a series.

Eyre: You should always defend if the attacker's actions will slow you down. If the attackers all go the same way, defend a lead. If they split up your defence becomes broken and you have to decide which group to cover. As often as not you are caught in the middle with both wings paying, and that's no use. It is essential to go all the way with one group or other, on whichever side you consider best. I will luff viciously on a reach to defend my weather, but I do it early, more as a deterrent than anything else. I will also gybe to get clear wind on a run. If I have to beat a particular boat to win a series, then I stick to him like glue.

Bruce: It is only worth defending if you are in first place; and then only to the extent of consolidating one's position in relation to the fleet. The exception is if you and the second boat are so far ahead of the fleet that there is no chance of them catching you.

McNamara: Depending on the size of the fleet, I don't see any harm in using the odd tack to cover as soon as possible, particularly if it means that I could go the right way. In the lead I would begin to cover three-quarters of the way up the first beat. I want to win and win well, and I've never wanted to win by stopping a rival. I've only once really covered to stop someone else by blotting him out of the last race of a series, and although I won that series, I never felt right about it.

Warren: I begin to defend on the second beat, by covering that is; I will defend my wind on a reach at any time. At the end of a series I will cover right from the starting line.

Oakeley: Defend as soon as you have established a lead, at least a reasonable lead, which is unlikely to be before three-quarters of the way up the first beat. With one race of a series to go, it is feasible to cover your major rival from the ten-minute gun; but you must be sure that you can finish down the fleet as well.

Crebbin: It's rarely that you need to employ defensive tactics up the first beat in a competitive fleet; the only time is when you are leading and getting near the windward mark. Then you should always keep between your opponents and the mark. Once off the wind, the fleet is in a defined order, and defence becomes as important as attack. When you should start serious defence definitely depends on where you are in relation to your main rivals. If you are behind, you have to go flat out to get ahead of them, but if you are ahead then you are probably not so worried about those in front. Once you are well into a series you must be aware of the overall position. Towards the end it is the series that must be your aim; the individual race position does not matter.

Batt: I defend from the first reach and always keep in touch with immediate threats. Defence is far harder in tight competition, but it is important to the overall result. You cannot afford to let your close rivals off the hook at any time.

What are the most important defensive tactics?

Eyre: Shadowing from the windward side, remaining between the following boat and the next mark, and the lee bow position are the three most important on the beats. Luffing and following a boat to leeward on the reaches and gybing to clear one's wind on the run are the offwind defence tactics I find important.

Peter White: Staying between the opposition and the next mark at all times on the beat and preventing the opposition from coming through to weather on the reaches.

Pattisson: Defence is really composed of covering, keeping your wind clear and staying between the next mark and the nearest boat behind you.

Reg White: In a catamaran the only real defence is to cover on the beats. The relative speeds on the downwind legs make defence almost impossible.

Jobbins: The beat is most important in sailing for defence. Once you are ahead you can control the race of those behind you. You can herd them whichever way you want them to go by tacking right on top of them and forcing them to the side of the course to which you want them to go. Maybe you have to encourage the boat behind you to cover the boat behind him and so on, but up the last beat in particular this

should not be too difficult.

Oakeley: The best way to stop a rival on the wind is to tack dead to windward of him. Sitting in disturbed air, he must lose ground. On a reach it is important to get your spinnaker set before the boat astern sets his and to keep your wind clear, by luffing if necessary.

Warren: Covering hard on the windward legs is often the only way to stay in front. It certainly is if the boat behind is faster. You can keep a faster boat back by covering, but there is always the risk that the rest of the fleet will pass you if the battle becomes too intense. On the reaches one method of defence is to stay well down to leeward and refuse to be drawn up with the luffing bunch. On the run it pays to run by the lee to get clear wind from a covering boat, because the attacker will have to gybe to get over your wind.

Bruce: You are far more likely to do better by trying to improve your position rather than protect it. Make any defensive moves that are necessary definite and pronounced so that an opponent knows that he is not passing a pussy-cat. Don't look behind on a reach, but concentrate on getting as much out of the boat as possible.

Crebbin: On any leg of the course the prime defensive tactic is boatspeed and teamwork. But there are times when these are not enough. Covering to windward depends on whether there is a large group of boats, a small group or an individual. Keeping ahead of a large group is a matter of loose cover only; the smaller the bunch you are covering, the tighter the cover becomes. Avoid covering one group of boats right out to one side of the course; keep your eye on the next group too. With a spinnaker up much can be lost by not concentrating on the speed of the boat. Keep to the straight line for as long as is possible without a boat on your wind; there is no harm in warning the boat astern that you do not intend to let him pass to windward by deliberately luffing a bit if he tries it on. Near the gybe mark, however, it is better that he should go to the weather side rather than establish an overlap. Without a spinnaker it is more important to avoid luffing out to weather too much. Don't luff one and lose two! Keep on the overlap side on the run and make the attacker run around to take your wind; you will then travel the shorter distance.

Batt: I try to stay in front rather than dead to windward on the beats; somehow I feel that this gives me greater control of the situation. Only when I want the man behind to tack to the other side of the course do I sit directly in his wind. On the reaches I try to force the boat behind me to leeward into my dirty wind and wash. I only luff if there is a lot at stake or there is a big gap behind. Clear air on the run is all-important, and it doesn't matter to me how many gybes I have to do to get it.

McNamara: If one covers hard on the beat, the man behind can start to dictate the tactics; in fact hard covering will encourage him to do so. Then you lose out to him. Loose cover and playing the shifts is preferable. Reaching is dominated by the boat behind; therefore clear air and protecting one's weather are all-important. On the run I am prepared to gybe any number of times to keep clear wind.

With the right-hand side of the course paying, the New Zealand Finn should now tack on to starboard and loose cover the two immediately behind him. He will not affect their wind but will remain in touch if there is a windshift.

Maynard: The general rule upwind is to stay between the next competitor and the mark. The question remains whether to loose cover or to keep him close. It is difficult to get an opponent into a close cover situation, because he will tack just as soon as you tack on him and then you lose him; another tack then would kill all your boatspeed. It is possible to get that position after the leeward mark by putting in a short hitch on starboard round the mark and then coming back on to port before the next boat gets to the mark, so that as it rounds you are dead upwind. But this means losing the ground of two tacks that the next boat doesn't have to make. Nor will he allow this close cover to go on for long – he will probably institute a tacking duel that will allow the boats behind to catch up. Therefore I only close cover when I know that the man behind is faster than me on the wind and that unless I cover him he will get past, or when the wind is very shifty, or when I want to force the boat on to the other tack.

If you have a large lead, you must plan to get dead to weather of the nearest boat, for there is much more to be lost by going out to one side if the wind shifts. If you are content that your opponent is on the correct tack and is sailing the course that you yourself want to sail, it is incorrect to tack on his wind so that he tacks and forces you to go the same way with him. Tack when you are just ahead of abeam so that his wind is clear. If you cross him by only a few boat lengths, however, this tactic is not safe because he could establish a lee bow on you. In that situation you would be better to tack to leeward of him so that you stay ahead but do not make him feel obliged to tack. If he is not on the tack on which you want him

then tack hard on his wind; this will encourage him to tack, and then follow him with a loose cover. In this way you can shepherd your nearest opponents in the direction you want them to go. The standard defence while reaching is to luff gently as the attacker approaches. If you luff too quickly you will lose too much distance; if you luff too slowly, he will be through; only luff sufficiently to protect your wind. Little can be done to prevent a boat from breaking through to leeward, except by sailing as low a course as is permitted by the rules. If anyone can break through your lee close to, then it's worth checking your rudder for weed!

Attempt to keep your wind clear on the run by luffing gently. A really determined attacker is bound to gain unless you start broad reaching away from the rhumb line. If he follows you and starts to take your wind, gybe back, and the process is reversed – great tactics unless there are other boats about. In a *Finn* with the boom squared off at more than 90 degrees to the centreline, it is possible to get safely down to leeward by running by the lee.

How do you deal with a slightly faster boat on a broad spinnaker reach when you are ahead?

Pattisson: On the first reach of an Olympic course, I would luff boldly and try to persuade the attacker to go to leeward. If this fails, I would allow the boat through rather than risk losing other places. I would do the same on the second reach, though I might be a little more determined to hold off someone faster if I were close to the buoy. On the final downwind leg of the course I might allow an attacker through if I were definitely faster upwind, but if I knew that I would have trouble on the final leg I would luff desperately to stay ahead.

    Maynard: If you are well ahead of the rest of the fleet and there is no chance of being caught by any of the boats astern, you must stop the other boat from coming through. If it is only marginally faster there is very little chance that it will be able to break through to leeward, and so the only worry is that it will break through to windward. An attacker will almost certainly go for your weather; at that point a gentle luff to keep clear wind will inform the attacking helmsman that he won't get past easily. On the first reach it is important to encourage the attacker to pass to windward by luffing just enough to keep your wind clear but not so hard that he makes an attempt to leeward, thereby establishing an overlap at the gybe mark. On the second reach much harder luffing at first will tend to drive an attacker to leeward. If there are boats close behind,

however, there is little point in employing these tactics too rigorously. In the early stages of a series it is advisable to let the other boat pass with a minimum of fuss.

    Batt: First of all I try not to look back but to concentrate on my own boatspeed; since I'm already ahead there is every chance that I can get ahead again, though I would encourage an attacker to take a leeward course by luffing.

    Crebbin: On the first reach I would begin by dropping below the course line, which would encourage the other boats to go to windward; by then I would have a little space in hand in which to luff and travel faster. By going low of the course line, there is more chance of breaking the overlap close to the mark by luffing, should the

US 611 will have to sail very high when she has completed her gybe to keep her wind clear. The dark-hulled boat ahead of her will control this situation.

other boat attack to leeward. On the second reach the attacking boat must be encouraged to leeward; it is relatively easy to make it clear that you will luff hard to protect your clear wind – if he really is faster he will not want to get involved in a luffing match. The later in the race this occurs, the more violent these tactics can be, particularly if there are not many other boats around. However, it is sometimes prudent to let one boat go so as to be certain of keeping ahead of another group.

Bruce: Go high if it's early on the first reach and force the other boat to leeward; close to the gybe mark the other boat must be encouraged to pass to windward and not get an overlap. On the second reach the attacker must be made to go to leeward.

Warren: My first worry is about my own boatspeed, because there's no real reason why any boat should be noticeably faster on a reach. Is there weed on the centreboard or rudder? Perhaps the spinnaker is poor. But I do not allow one boat to cloud my judgement of my overall race plan. It is far more important to look at the race as a whole rather than be taken out by some side issue.

Oakeley: I would ignore a boat going faster and endeavour to catch him on the next leg. If another boat is noticeably faster, there is little that one can do to hold it off without detriment to one's own position.

Jobbins: I try to make sure that the other boat is forced to leeward so that he has to sail in a load of dirty wind.

Reg White: It depends entirely on what the other boats around are doing.

Peter White: Force the other boat to leeward, except near the gybe mark, where the inside berth is all important.

Eyre: If the race were shortened at

the end of a reach I would luff the attacker hard rather than let him pass to windward. In most other situations the attacker must be encouraged to leeward, but not at the expense of losing other places.

Should use of the right-of-way rule be pushed to the limit in defence?

Warren: I often think that it is better to let a port tack boat go across when you could in fact claim a foul – there may well be a time when he might do the same for you.

Reg White: Not if it puts your own boat in danger.

Jobbins: Only when rounding marks.

Batt: Of course the rules should be used to their limits, but I don't believe in going round hitting people. I don't like protests or disqualifications, but if it is possible to manoeuvre other boats to my advantage then I will use the rules to do so.

McNamara: I use the rules right up to the full stop. It's the only way – otherwise areas of grey develop and doubts creep in. For example, if I were the outside boat on a dead run well to port of a group of other boats I would have no hesitation in gybing on to starboard, forcing the others to gybe and going away from the mark so that when I gybed on to port I could break the overlap.

Crebbin: All tactics are bound by the rules, so it is important to get as much out of them as you can. One should use a double gybe to re-establish luffing rights after they are broken, without having to get clear ahead.

Eyre: I don't think that one should

As the right-hand side of the course works best in Weymouth Bay during the 1974 World Championship, G 1288 controls the fleet. No one can tack until G 1288 has gone about and she will have clear wind.

152

use the rules to the point of causing a collision that will slow one down. After all the rules are framed to prevent collision and there seems little point in causing unnecessary damage.

Oakeley: The introduction of the 720-degree turn has encouraged minor fouling in defence. This is not good, but nonetheless I think that the rules have to be used to their limits.

Maynard: It is all very well to push right-of-way rules to their limits in team racing, but in championships and other serious racing it is very rarely worth the risk. If you take the rules to what you consider to be the limits, the chances are that the other guy won't have the same opinion, and this could well lead to a collision and an unnecessary visit to the protest room. In a championship series a protest is very serious because of the stress and uncertainty that it causes, especially if the protest is not heard on the same day as the incident occurred. Also, international juries are often scraped together from people of different nationalities and of doubtful experience. Some juries can be blatantly nationalistic and others allow international politics to creep in. Thus what looks like a cast-iron case to the protestor can often end as a travesty of justice. During important championship races the golden rule should be 'stay out of trouble'. The problem areas are claiming water at a mark close to the two boat length area, lee bow tacks, tacking close especially from port to starboard and from boats in close proximity at the starting line.

Pattisson: One has to use the rules to the limits but not to the point of a collision. I would only risk a collision on a blatant case of port and starboard, and if this resulted in a protest I would make sure that my evidence showed that I had attempted to avoid the collision at all costs. I prefer to win on boatspeed rather than on the rules; one can never be sure what false evidence an opponent will dream up in the protest room.

Bruce: The rules are made to govern the sport and should therefore be used, but not so that you start in any way to infringe sportsmanship and the pure pleasure of sailing. At no time should two competitors team up to stop a third in normal racing.

Peter White: Right-of-way rules are always worth enforcing at marks and on the finish line, but not necessarily in the middle of the course, where it is sometimes better to waive the right of way. For instance, it is often best to allow a port tack boat to cross ahead by bearing away slightly rather than having it tack on your own lee bow.

At the start of the final beat there is one boat fifteen seconds astern at the last mark. How do you plan this final leg?

Pattisson: If my windward boatspeed is the same as my opponent's or perhaps faster, I would cover him loosely. If I know I am slower and the other boats are well behind I would cover the other boat dead to windward and attempt to keep him there at all costs.

Oakeley: No matter what the boat astern does it is important to stay with it. Your defence should be to keep between the other boat and the finishing line, being careful that you are not taken out to the lay-line. Your opponent is likely to instigate a tacking duel in an effort to force you into a mistake. This is the time in the race when you are most tired, and it is therefore necessary to be more careful

154

and more vigilant than ever before.

Crebbin: If you and he are the only two boats with a chance of winning the race, then the cover should be very close indeed. It is frustrating for the leeward boat because by sailing in disturbed air it is necessarily going slower. If there are other boats sufficiently close then you should endeavour to shepherd the nearest boat by loose covering into covering those astern. If one side of the beat is preferable then you must shepherd your opponent out to that side as well. If for some reason your opponent tacks better, do not cover dead to windward as you will get involved in a tacking duel which will result in the gap being narrowed.

Bruce: Give your opponent an opening toward the side of the course that you want to go, then tack with a loose cover and try to observe whether

he is tacking on the lifting shifts. If you are certain that he is, let him alone. It takes guts to do so, but you will almost certainly lose out if you cover him in these conditions. Otherwise cover tightly when the boat sails away from the favoured side of the course and only loosely when he sails towards it.

Peter White: Try to keep between your opponent and the finish without covering tightly. This will ensure that you will go fast up the final leg without getting involved in time-consuming tacking duels, protected from the rest of the opposition.

Eyre: Unless the opposing boat is accompanied by others I would cover him very closely.

McNamara: I would stay

K 321 is forced into a tight rounding of this leeward mark and that could momentarily reduce her speed. K 284 could then drive through her lee. However, 284 has to give 321 sufficient room to round the mark, and the skipper of 321 should not be forced into this error.

between my opponent and the windward mark. If he were going slightly faster I would sacrifice some of my lead to bear away and cover hard. The more the boat behind tacks, the fewer advantages its better boatspeed will bring it; the more it tries to bear to drive through the leader's dirty wind, the less chance it has. Once both boats get out onto the lay-line the attacker has even bigger problems.

Batt: Cover loosely; then the boat behind will have less incentive to dictate the tactics. The boat behind should try to stay in the middle of the course. In the lead the best bet is to get to the lay-line with the boat behind covered – then the attacker will have no chance.

Maynard: The only way of getting dead to windward of the next boat is by putting in two tacks before it rounds the leeward mark. With a lead of fifteen seconds, this is just not possible. If, after rounding the mark, it is necessary to get onto starboard tack quickly, the boat behind can be forced onto that tack by the leader pointing very high and forcing the boat behind to fall off to leeward. The attacker will then feel obliged to tack, and when he goes the leader should tack and maintain a loose cover. If the leader is worried about the speed of the attacker, he can sail fast and free to get dead to windward. If it's best to stay on port tack after rounding the leeward mark, sail fast and a little free so that it appears that you are not interfering with the wind of the boat behind. When the boat behind finally does tack onto starboard it is important for the leader to go with him and maintain a loose cover.

Jobbins: If the boat behind is faster then it is essential for the leader to cover hard all the way to the finish.

Warren: With a narrow lead it's not possible to get dead to windward of the boat behind immediately; it is therefore all the more important to round the last mark well, approaching it wide and hardening up close, so that the boat behind is forced into the leader's disturbed wind. It is generally best to cover only by sailing in the same direction and not get involved in a tacking duel, which might present dangers from a third boat.

A twenty-second lead at the last mark over a bunch of four boats is a different problem. How do you deal with that?

Maynard: The boats behind will be almost certain to split tacks. Then the leader must decide which is the correct way to go up the windward leg. If it is better to go to the port side, the leader should sail fast and free away from the mark so that those closest will be encouraged to go the same way; conversely, if he decides to go to starboard it is essential to claw high, forcing those immediately behind to tack. Generally speaking it usually pays to hold on for a while on port tack on the final beat because the boats running into the leeward mark cause an area of disturbed wind, and any boats tacking onto starboard into that area will be slowed up. Shepherding tactics will probably not work with four boats if they are all sailing aggressively. The important thing is to decide on the best initial tack after the mark and to encourage the leading boat to stay with you. Fairly hard covering among the boats in the pursuing pack is likely, and this should make them reduce their aggression.

Warren: It is quite possible that the groups of boats astern will be so concerned with holding their position that they will all go in roughly the same direction; this makes the leader's job much easier. But with so many boats in close contention the leader must be careful to tack on the right shifts, because one of the boats behind will undoubtedly do so and can easily pull back this much in a couple of tacks. It is essential to cover those boats which go in the direction the leader feels is best.

Eyre: I would be forced to cover those sailing on the favoured side of the course.

Jobbins: Generally, herding will make the situation relatively easy for the leader. If, however, the group separates, then you must cover the quickest of your pursuers and endeavour to force him to go the right way.

Peter White: Loose cover the nearest boat, making sure that you choose the right windshifts.

Reg White: With a catamaran it is important not to be forced into tacking too often; it is far better to use the windshifts to advantage and only cover hard with the finish line in sight.

McNamara: If there is an established right of way up the final beat, then the situation will probably be eased by one or maybe two of the others going the opposite way looking for a flyer. The leader must loose cover the closest boat, but because the pursuing bunch is not close enough for him to cover them all, it is important to play the windshifts. It's easy to lose twenty seconds by just trying not to lose.

Bruce: If I ever become involved in this situation I do it very badly. I prefer to sail my own race heading for the favoured side of the course, where the sensible ones will go anyway.

Oakeley: The only way to cover four boats at the same time is to make

them all go the same way. The leader must make his nearest challengers go the same way as the remainder of the bunch. If the leading boats in pursuit try to split away, it is important to give them as much dirty wind as possible so that they tack back into the herd. Then the leader's cover must be loose.

Crebbin: When leading you must decide which of the bunch is the most dangerous; overall positions in the series are particularly important. The leader should keep between the finish and as many of the group as he can. In a fast-tacking boat it is possible with a lead of twenty seconds to put in two tacks after rounding the mark and get dead to windward of the opposition. From this position it is possible to control the herding. If there are more than four boats in the group astern the leader should concentrate on sailing straight to the finish using the windshifts rather than on manoeuvring the other boats.

Batt: There may be some in-fighting in the bunch astern which must help the leader. If the pursuing bunch splits up I would cover those in the bunch that most threatened me and the overall standings.

Pattisson: I would sail as fast a course to the finishing line as I could, keeping a watch on the situation at the same time. When the boats separate I would start loose covering the one that becomes the clear leader, continuing to watch the progress of the others. If they all go the other way you have to force your opponent to try to break cover and go after the rest of the bunch.

Are there other minor defensive tactics?

Peter White: The best defence is to keep clear of incidents whenever possible. It never pays to pull a fast one,

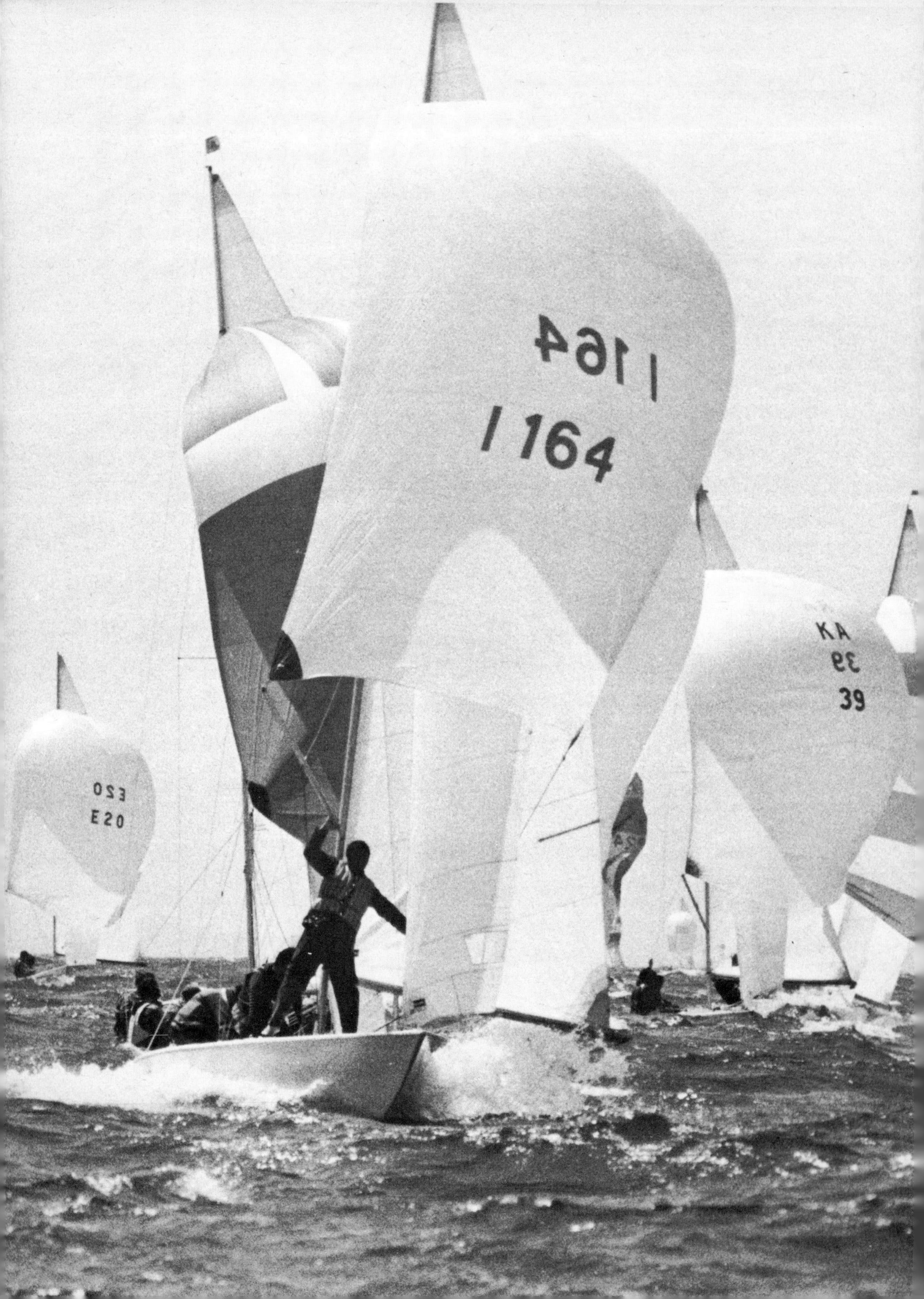
I 164
KA
39
E20

because the move will almost always be reciprocated. Getting involved in personal duels is costly to both parties.

Warren: The best defence is attack. Once you concentrate on defence you are at a disadvantage. The worst mistake is to try to gain 'vanity time' near the finish to improve on an already good lead.

Crebbin: Personal relationships play an important part. If you gain a reputation for bad sportsmanship it will make people pick you rather than anyone else to cover out of a group of boats. You must not allow personal desire to beat an opponent ruin your overall chances of winning a series.

Maynard: Too many people throw away places in a race by incorrect covering close to the finishing line. Once the leading boat is approaching the finish, a skipper should stop covering and concentrate on finishing at the right end of the line. The second boat usually attempts a few desperate tacks near the finish in the hope of getting the boat ahead to make a mistake. If the leading boat slavishly covers it can end up finishing up at the upwind end of the line or overstanding the finish altogether.

Batt: Perhaps the best defence-mechanism is self-confidence and a level head. If you've won a lead there is no reason not to keep it. If you take the lead on the first beat there is no reason why the final beat should be any less manageable. In front, it is easier to be cautious; behind, it is easier to be aggressive. Continuing aggression while in the lead is the best defence of all.

I 164 is almost at the mark and has come in wide enough for a good rounding, so that she can sail high early on the next reach to protect her weather.

Conclusions
Chapter 17

It is dedication that is common to all the champions who have contributed to this book. Without meticulous attention to detail there will be no success, and such attention must begin long before the boat ever goes into the water. The majority of races can be won or lost ashore, generally by neglect. A true champion will rarely have gear failure. Gear failures increase the further down the fleet you go. But it is not necessary to have the brightest, shiniest, newest and most expensive of toys to win races. Winning boats are workmanlike, with no concessions to frills or fancies; everything has a purpose and, above all, everything works. For the top small-boat sailor his boat becomes an extension of his arms and legs; his reactions are instinctive, and the champion's are instinctively right.

It was Paul Elvström's almost slavish devotion to physical fitness that revolutionized small-boat sailing. Sailing a *Firefly* in the single-handed class at the 1948 Olympics in Torbay, he found that he could pass several boats in the later stages of the race because he was still capable of sitting out while his rivals wilted. His other, almost obsessive, mania was to sail his boat as much as was possible; he became so familiar with it that he could handle it automatically. It is no coincidence, therefore, that his name appears more frequently in the lists of Olympic and World Champions at the end of this book than any other. And what is more, almost every one of the champions who have contributed to this book have been influenced by Elvström's thinking.

Each class develops its gear and equipment, sails and spars slightly differently. Nonetheless there is a tremendous amount of overspill from one class to another and top sailors from all classes can often be found wandering around the dinghy parks at championship events looking at the new ideas. Pure plagiarism is not enough, however; by all means copy someone else's idea, if it is good, but it is far better to make that idea work even more efficiently. Of course some ideas are only applicable to one particular class; the boat may need a particular style of gear to suit its hull shape or its rig. There is nothing so stultifying as failure to explore new possibilities. When Joan Ellis and her husband Art, who crews for her, became the *Fireball* champions of 1975, the setup of their rig was very different from that of any of their rivals. This was not because most of the physical strength came from crewman Art – in fact, some of their ideas put more strain on Joan than a conventional rig might have done. But their rig was more efficient and flexible and could be worked more quickly than any of their competitors'. It has brought about a re-think in the entire class.

Opposition can be destroyed by the skipper who thinks ahead. In 1968 Rodney Pattisson took an articulated centreboard to the Mexico Olympics. He had kept it secret until then and it caused so big an outcry from his rivals that an extraordinary meeting of the class association banned it. Whether it worked or not was another matter, but it gave Pattisson a psychological advantage over all his rivals at those Games. What happened there is now part of yachting history: he was disqualified for an infringement on the starting-line of the first race, won the

160

next five races in a row and was second in the final race, taking the Gold Medal by the largest-ever margin in the history of the yachting Olympics.

In tactical sailing, champions are aggressive towards the elements and respect their fellow-competitors. Their policy is to stay out of trouble; they rely on their ability to get or to stay ahead rather than risk a possible disqualification. Small-boat racing does not have referees or umpires and how far the rules are observed is largely up to the competitors themselves. Almost everyone sails fairly; anyone who doesn't is quickly found out and ostracized. There is less bad sportsmanship in sailing than in any sport, purely because the responsibility for playing straight is entirely the competitors.

To compete with the champions first find out what put them there: in every case a well-prepared boat, excellent co-ordination, fitness and, above all, desire to win. Without any of these the route to the top is almost impossible. Above all, every champion really enjoys his sailing. Many champions are often attacked for their commercial involvement with small boats. As the sport has expanded more sailmakers, more boat-builders and more fitting manufacturers have set up business.

Many of these, in fact the vast majority, were sailors first and now earn their living because they have something to offer a commercial concern. They benefit mainly because they have time to sail. But there is no reason why the dedicated small-boat sailor who earns his living outside yachting should not be able to compete on equal terms. It does demand extra dedication to the sport, but no more than that required for success at the top in any field.

Winning may not be everything. Losing is nothing.

Olympic and World Championship results

Olympic Medallists
Finn

1952 1. Paul Elvström (Denmark)
      2. Charles Currey (Great Britain)
      3. Rickard Sarby (Sweden)
1956 1. Paul Elvström (Denmark)
      2. André Nelis (Belgium)
      3. John Marvin (USA)
1960 1. Paul Elvström (Denmark)
      2. Aleksandr Tschutschelov (USSR)
      3. André Nelis (Belgium)
1964 1. Willi Kuhweide (West Germany)
      2. Peter Barrett (USA)
      3. Henning Wind (Denmark)
1968 1. Valentin Mankin (USSR)
      2. Hubert Raudaschl (Austria)
      3. Fabio Albarelli (Italy)
1972 1. Serge Maury (France)
      2. Ilias Hatzipavlias (Greece)
      3. Viktor Potapov (USSR)

Flying Dutchman

1960 1. Peder Lunde and Bjorn Bergvall
        (Norway)
      2. Hans Fogh and Ole Petersen
        (Denmark)
      3. Rolf Mulka and Ingo von Bredow
        (West Germany)
1964 1. Helmer Pederson and Earle Wells
        (New Zealand)
      2. Keith Musto and Tony Morgan
        (Great Britain)
      3. Buddy Melges and Bill Bentsen
        (USA)
1968 1. Rodney Pattisson and Iain
        Macdonald-Smith (Great Britain)
      2. Uli Libor and Peter Naumann
        (West Germany)
      3. Reinaldo Conrad and Burkhard
        Cordes (Brazil)
1972 1. Rodney Pattisson and Chris Davies
        (Great Britain)
      2. Yves and Marc Pajot (France)
      3. Uli Libor and Peter Naumann
        (West Germany)

Tempest

1972 1. Valentin Mankin and Vitalii
        Dyrdyra (USSR)
      2. Alan Warren and David Hunt
        (Great Britain)
      3. Glen Foster and Peter Dean (USA)

Soling

1972 1. Buddy Melges, Bill Bentsen and
        Bill Allen (USA)
      2. Stig Wennerstrom, Stefan Krook
        and Bo Knape (Sweden)
      3. David Miller, Paul Coté
        and John Ekles (Canada)

World Champions
505

1956 Jacques le Brun (France)
1957 Paul Elvström (Denmark)
1958 Paul Elvström (Denmark)
1959 Marcel Buffet (France)
1960 Marcel Buffet (France)
1961 André Cornu (France)
1962 Keith Paul (Great Britain)
1963 Bryan Farren-Price (Australia)
1964 John Parrington (Australia)
1965 Derek Farrant (Great Britain)
1966 Jim Hardy (Australia)
1967 Bertrand Moret (France)
1968 Marcel Troudel (France)
1969 Larry Marks (Great Britain)
1970 Larry Marks (Great Britain)
1971 Derek Farrant (Great Britain)
1972 Nicholas Loday (France)
1973 Peter White (Great Britain)
1974 Yves Pajot (France)
1975 John Loveday (Great Britain)

International Moth

1963 Bill Schill (USA)
1964 Jean-Pierre Roggo (Switzerland)
1965 Jean-Pierre Roggo (Switzerland)
1966 Jean-Pierre Roggo (Switzerland)
1967 Blair Fletcher (USA)
1968 Marie-Claud Faroux (France)
1969 Dave McKay (Australia)
1970 Dave McKay (Australia)
1971 Jacques Faroux (France)
1972 Jacques Faroux (France)
1973 Ian Brown (Australia)
1974 Rob O'Sullivan (Australia)
1975 Peter Moor (Australia)

Tempest

1967 Cliff Norbury (Great Britain)
1968 Bill Kelly (USA)
1969 Cliff Norbury (Great Britain)
1970 John Linville (USA)
1971 Glen Foster (USA)

1972 not held
1973 Valentin Mankin (USSR)
1974 Uwe Mares (West Germany)
1975 Guiseppe Milone (Italy)

Flying Dutchman
1956 Rolf Mulka (West Germany)
1957 Rolf Mulka (West Germany)
1958 Rolly Tasker (Australia)
1959 Mario Capio (Italy)
1960 not held
1961 not held
1962 Hans Fogh (Denmark)
1963 Jean-Pierre Renvier (Switzerland)
1964 not held
1965 Dick Pitcher (Great Britain)
1966 not held
1967 John Oakeley (Great Britain)
1968 not held
1969 Rodney Pattisson (Great Britain)
1970 Rodney Pattisson (Great Britain)
1971 Rodney Pattisson (Great Britain)
1972 not held
1973 Hans Fogh (Canada)
1974 Ilja Wolf (East Germany)
1975 Yves Pajot (France)

Laser
1974 Peter Commette (USA)
1975 not held

Soling
1969 Paul Elvström (Denmark)
1970 Stig Wennerstrom (Sweden)
1971 Robert Mosbacher (USA)
1972 not held
1973 Ib Andersen (Denmark)
1974 Paul Elvström (Denmark)
1975 Bill Buchan (USA)

Finn (Gold Cup)
1956 André Nelis (Belgium)
1957 Jurgen Vogler (East Germany)
1958 Paul Elvström (Denmark)
1959 Paul Elvström (Denmark)
1960 Vernon Stratton (Great Britain)
1961 André Nelis (Belgium)
1962 Arne Akerson (Sweden)
1963 Willi Kuhweide (West Germany)
1964 Hubert Raudaschl (Austria)
1965 Jurgen Mier (East Germany)
1966 Willi Kuhweide (West Germany)
1967 Willi Kuhweide (West Germany)
1968 Henning Wind (Denmark)
1969 Thomas Lundquist (Sweden)
1970 Jorg Bruder (Brazil)
1971 Jorg Bruder (Brazil)
1972 Jorg Bruder (Brazil)

1973 Serge Maury (France)
1974 Henry Sprague (USA)
1975 Magnus Olin (Sweden)
1976 Chris Law (Great Britain)

470
1970 Carré (France)
1971 Van Essen (Holland)
1972 Vollebregt (Holland)
1973 Soderlund (Denmark)
1974 Gorestegui (Spain)
1975 Marc Laurent (France)

Enterprise
1970 Roger Hance (Great Britain)
1971 Paul McNamara (Great Britain)
1972 Roger Hance (Great Britain)
1973 Peter Byrne (Canada)
1974 Philip Crebbin (Great Britain)
1975 Michael Holmes (Great Britain)

Tornado
1968 Ian Tremlett (Great Britain)
1969 Maurie Davie (Australia)
1970 Paul Lindenberg (USA)
1971 Ian Fraser (Great Britain)
1972 Robert Jessenig (Austria)
1973 Bruce Stewart (USA)
1974 Robert Jessenig (Austria)
1975 Jorg Spengler (West Germany)
1976 Reg White (Great Britain)

OK
1963 Svend Jacobsen (Denmark)
1964 Henning Schntchtshabei (Denmark)
1965 Goeran Andersson (Sweden)
1966 Goeran Andersson (Sweden)
1967 Bjorn Arnesson (Sweden)
1968 Erik Fromell (Sweden)
1969 Kent Carlsson (Sweden)
1970 Kent Carlsson (Sweden)
1971 Thomas Jungblut (West Germany)
1972 Kjell Axerop (Sweden)
1973 Clive Roberts (New Zealand)
1974 Torben Andrup (Denmark)
1975 Paul Kirketerp (Denmark)

Fireball
1966 Bob Fisher (Great Britain)
1967 Peter Bateman (Great Britain)
1968 Peter Bateman (Great Britain)
1969 not held
1970 John Caig (Great Britain)
1971 John Caig (Great Britain)
1972 Jorg Diesch (West Germany)
1973 Kenneth Brackwell (Great Britain)
1974 John Cassidy (Australia)
1975 Joan Ellis (USA)

The international racing rules explained

The International Racing Rules are arranged in six parts. Part I is composed entirely of definitions. Part II deals with the management of races and the authority and duties of a race committee. The owner's responsibility for qualifying his yacht forms most of the general requirements set out in Part III. The essential right-of-way rules are laid down in Part IV, and the other sailing rules, concerning the obligations of the helmsman and crew in handling the boat, form Part V. Part VI deals with protests, disqualifications and appeals.

The definitions set out in Part I must be fully understood: it is on them that the whole structure of the rules is based. All too often people get into difficulties and find themselves on the wrong side of a protest meeting because they have failed to get a firm grasp of the fundamentals. The definitions are clear, and any term defined in Part I appears in bold type when used in its defined sense elsewhere in the rules.

A race, a series of races or a regatta must have a distinct form, and this form is standardized in Part II. The management of races and the way in which they are run is laid down in rules 1 to 14. Rule 1 concerns the general authority of a race committee and the officials responsible for organizing racing; it sets out the basic limitations on the organizers and allows them to reject any entry without stating the reason. Rules 2 and 3 deal with the notice of a race and the sailing instructions which supplement the International Racing Rules. The standardization of code flag signals,

which eliminate a great deal of error in communication between the race committee and the competitors, is dealt with by Rule 4, while other signals and the race committee's duties are covered in the rest of Part II. Rule 12 – 'Yacht Materially Prejudiced', is one of the rules most used by competitors if they are fouled or damaged by another boat. A protest made under Rule 12 can result in the race being cancelled or abandoned; or the protestor may be given a higher place than the one in which he finished, at the judgement of the race committee.

Part III deals with the competitor's obligations before racing. Rule 18 covers the form of entry, rule 19 measurement certificates. Each boat entering a race must hold a valid measurement or rating certificate as required by any authority having bearing on the race, whether a national authority, the class rules, or even the sailing instructions. It is the owner's responsibility to maintain the boat in the condition on which the certificate was based. Rule 22 deals with shifting ballast, in general banning its use, and with the clothing and equipment competitors may wear. Safety is covered in rules 23 and 24; every boat must carry an anchor of suitable size and life-saving equipment for each person on board.

Rule 26 is concerned with advertisements. To comply with the similarly numbered rule of the International Olympic Committee which defines amateur status the IYRU rules state that no part of the hull or crew or equipment of a boat shall display any form of advertisement. The exceptions concern sailmakers'

The helmsman of 19047 will have to take care not to foul the right of way, starboard tack, 19307. But 19074 will easily clear right of way boat 19147.

trademarks and the builder's plate, the size of which is limited to 150 mm by 150 mm. This rule precludes semi-professional skiff-racing, which is becoming increasingly popular throughout the world, from amateur status, because almost every boat has a sponsor and carries its sponsor's mark or name on the sails.

Rules 31 to 46 form Part IV of the rules and concern the helmsman's rights and obligations when two yachts meet. To make things simple, this Part is broken down under six headings. The first section consists of rules which *always* apply and deals with dis-qualification, avoiding collisions, retiring from a race, the right of way of a yacht altering course and hailing when altering course in close proximity. The next two sections contain the fundamental rules. Section B, which consists only of rule 36, is the most important of all. It states that the starboard-tack yacht has right of way over a port-tack yacht. Section C (rules 37 to 40) deals with yachts on the same tack and with the rights and obligations of a yacht which luffs.

Rule 41 forms section D and governs the obligations of a boat tacking or gybing and of boats in close proximity to her.

Section E consists of rules of exception and special application; these deal with any of the rules in Part IV which may conflict with one another, except those in section A which always apply. Number 42 carefully outlines the rules concerning rounding marks or obstructions to sea room, and Rule 43 deals with the obligations of boats hailing and hailed for room to tack at obstructions when close hauled. The obligation of a premature starter to keep clear of the rest of the boats racing is

laid down in Rule 44, with the rider that until it is obvious that such a boat is returning to start again she shall be accorded the rights of a yacht which has started. Rule 45 places similar obligations and rights on a boat re-rounding a mark after touching it. The final section, again of one rule only, deals with the rights of boats which are anchored, aground or capsized.

The rules set out in Part V are only enforced while a yacht is actually racing. The exception is Rule 49, entitled Fair Sailing, which discourages bad sportsmanship. It is worth quoting in full here.

A yacht shall attempt to win a race only by fair sailing, superior speed and skill, and, except in team races, by individual effort. However, a yacht may be disqualified under this rule only in the case of a clear-cut violation of the above principles and only if no other rule applies.

Rules 51 and 52 describe how the course shall be sailed and what happens if a boat touches a mark. The rest of Part V consists of minor regulations, although Rule 60 – Means of Propulsion – is an important one for dinghy-sailors. It is under this rule that protests have been lodged against competitors who continuously pump their sails contrary to Appendix 2 of the Rules. One of the purposes of the rule is to prevent a helmsman 'fanning' his boat around the course in light weather by flapping the sail, as a bird does its wing in flight. The important phrase in this rule is 'the natural action of the wind on the sails . . . . and water on the

The starting gun must have fired to allow US 564 to luff higher than a close hauled course. Before the start any luff must be carried out slowly and under Rule 40 'the leeward yacht shall not so luff above a close hauled course'.

hull'. Rule 65 was deliberately introduced to save yachtsmen money; it bans the release of any substance which could reduce the frictional resistance of the hull by altering the character of the flow of water inside the boundary layer. Such substances, polymers for instance, do exist, but they are very expensive.

The rules of Part VI deal with protests and penalties. Rule 67 places the onus on the helmsman of any boat which makes contact with another to retire or protest. If contact takes place and neither boat retires or protests, both are disqualified. The helmsman of a third yacht who witnesses a collision is entitled to protest against both parties and is relieved from flying a protest flag. Rule 74 allows national authorities to disqualify a competitor who has grossly infringed the rules, for any period, from

either steering or sailing in a yacht in any race held under its jurisdiction. Swearing at the race committee could result in a competitor being excluded from further participation in a series or for a longer period.

The rules are framed to avoid collisions between boats and to give equal opportunities to all competitors. When bias is required, right of way is given to the most skilful. For example, a boat which is just able to lay the windward mark close hauled does not have to give way to a boat inside it which cannot get round the mark without tacking, even though the two are overlapped. If the inside boat does hail for water to tack, it must retire immediately after receiving it.

Approaching the gybe mark US 564 has right of way over all yachts to windward, principally BL 33 and OE 48.